The
Life
and
Legend
of
George
McJunkin:
Black Cowboy

George McJunkin.

The Life and Legend of George McJunkin: *Black Cowboy*

by Franklin Folsom

illustrated with photographs

publishers since 1798

THOMAS NELSON INC.
NASHVILLE / NEW YORK

ACKNOWLEDGMENTS

The verse on p. 23 is from *Cowboy Lore* (1971), by Jules V. Allen. Reprinted by permission of The Naylor Company.

"Roundup's On," on pp. 103, 105 is from *Lost Trails of the Cimarron,* 3rd ed., by Harry E. Chrisman. Published by Swallow Press Inc., 1973. Reprinted by permission of the author.

First edition

Library of Congress Cataloging in Publication Data

Folsom, Franklin,
    The life and legend of George McJunkin.

    SUMMARY: A biography of the black cowboy whose skill with horses was renowned and whose curiosity led him to discover important archaeological relics.
    Bibliography: p.
    1. McJunkin, George—Juvenile literature. 2. Cowboys—Juvenile literature. [1. McJunkin, George. 2. Cowboys. 3. Negroes—Biography]
I. Title.
F596.M145F6   917.89'23 [B] [92]   73-6446
ISBN 0-8407-6326-3

CONTENTS

Bones, a Spear,
and a Search

One August afternoon in 1927, a man drove a team of horses as fast as they could pull a wagon along a rutted country road toward a small railway station in northern New Mexico. He was hurrying to put a letter on the evening train to Denver.

The letter, which was addressed to the Colorado Museum of Natural History, caused quite a stir when it arrived, and the museum's director dashed off telegrams to important scientists all over the country. Some of the scientists immediately dropped what they were doing and headed by train or automobile for the Crowfoot Ranch, eight miles outside the little town of Folsom, New Mexico. What they said when they got there made headlines in newspapers across the land.

The cause of all the excitement was this: The driver of the wagon, Carl Schwachheim, had made a discovery proving that eminent scientists in America were wrong on a subject of great general interest.

9

Close-up view of the famous Folsom point in its original form.

They had been insisting that the Indians came to America no more than three thousand years ago. What Carl had found, however, showed that people had lived in America for many, many thousands of years. The story of human life in the New World was much longer—and much more interesting—than all these learned experts had dared to think was possible.

Carl's discovery was actually a very small, very simple object — the stone tip of a spear — that had been buried under ten feet of soil, between two ribs in the skeleton of an unusually large bison. Some hunter long ago had made the spear thrust that killed the bison and then, possibly, after eating his fill of meat, had abandoned the carcass with the spearpoint still inside it. There it lay while rain-washed earth covered it deeper every year, century after century.

A skeleton, a spearpoint, ten feet of overlying earth — with only that much evidence a few bold scientists made a great breakthrough in puzzling out the hidden truth about the past of man in America. Just how they did it was a piece of detective work that is part of the story of this book.

But first, what about the discovery itself? How did Carl Schwachheim happen to dig up an ancient Indian's buried weapon?

That story begins, not with Carl, but with a young black boy, born a slave in Texas, who, after the Civil War, rode off alone one day across the prairie in search of freedom on the frontier.

In northern New Mexico near the Crowfoot Ranch, this black came to be known as the best rider and roper in that part of the country. His name was George McJunkin, but whites referred to him as Nigger George. No one was better than he at gentling wild broncs, and he could shoot straighter, fiddle longer, and spin a better yarn than anyone around. He studied the stars. He knew about wind and weather. Very little escaped his keen eyes, and he managed to find his way in terrible blizzards. In an area where most cowboys were from the South, this black onetime slave became foreman over whites on the Crowfoot Ranch.

It was George McJunkin who first discovered the ancient bones on the Crowfoot—bones that later made scientific history. A mature man then but still in search of freedom, George was to become in time an almost legendary figure. His life, and the legend, as told and retold by his friends in the years since his death, have been put together in the pages of this book.

CHAPTER 1

Hoo-Yah!
Ride 'Em!

Little beads of nervous sweat made George's skin glisten in the sunlight as he perched on the crossbar above the gate to the log corral. Milling around below were two dozen of Old Master McJunkin's half-broken horses. Any moment now one of the slave boys would open the gate, and the horses would surge through beneath George's dangling feet.

Could he make himself dive onto the back of one of those plunging mustangs?

Would he land squarely, sitting up straight, the way the older boys did? What if he fell off? He'd be cut to pieces by the sharp hooves.

"Ready?" cried Sam, who was holding the gate.

Sam had leaped many times onto the backs of half-wild horses, to ride off in triumph across the pasture—always when Mr. McJunkin and his white cowboys weren't watching. But George was scared. Sam, he kept thinking, was bigger and older.

Still, that was no excuse. Sam had started dropping

from the crossbar when he was ten. George was already a little past ten. Besides, he never had as hard a time sneaking a ride as Sam used to have. These days Mr. McJunkin spent very little time at the corral. Except for his slaves, he had no help around his big ranch on the San Antonio Road. All his white cowboys had gone off to fight for the South in the Civil War that had just broken out.

Sam swung the gate open, and a big gray horse wheeled and started through. The others followed, jostling and snorting in their rush for freedom. George tightened his grip on the crossbar. He wanted to close his eyes. His bare feet felt heavy, like stones.

The horses pushed and shouldered one another, and a little pinto paused as he found himself wedged between a large chestnut and a larger bay. This gave George his chance.

He held his breath, the way he did when he dived into the creek near Rogers Prairie, and suddenly shoved off.

He came down, bellywhopper, sprawled out on the pinto's back. But somehow he managed to clamp his legs against the sleek hide and to grab a fistful of mane with each hand.

Startled by the sudden weight on his back, the little horse stood in his tracks while the others rushed past him. Then he shook all over as if to get rid of flies, and the next thing George knew his mount was racing off across the pasture.

"Hoo-yah! Ride 'em!" Sam yelled.

George felt sure of himself now. He had often stolen rides on horses that had been gentled, even galloped them out across the pasture. But the ride today was different. It was a victory ride. This time he'd dared to leap onto a horse that was hardly rough-broke. And it had accepted him instead of bucking him off into the dust.

When the pinto caught up with his familiar grazing companions, he stopped and began to nibble at clumps of short spring grass. Still trembling a little, George slid to the ground and gave a good-bye swat to the horse's rump. In all his ten years—ten years spent as a slave among slaves—he had never felt so good.

"You did all right," Sam called out as George came back to the corral.

The words made George proud, but he couldn't stop to talk and hope for more praise. He had promised to help in his father's shop. His father was a blacksmith who pounded hot iron into horseshoes. Often George helped him by pumping air onto the bed of coals that heated the hard black iron and turned it red at first, then orange-white and soft.

There would be chances for more rides, George knew, but he did not realize how good the chances were going to be. For four years there were no white cowboys around. Service in the Confederate Army kept them away from home until 1865.

When the war ended, only a few of the survivors straggled back along the San Antonio Road to Rogers Prairie. In the meantime, during the years they were gone, George had learned how to do their work.

Mexican cowboys, who lived on a ranch not far away, taught him the things he wanted to know—how to swing a rope and drop a loop over a horse's head or how to snap a loop up under its heels. The Mexicans had been cowboys long before any white men from the States began to handle Texas longhorns. They and their fathers and grandfathers had herded cattle in the old days when Texas was a part of Mexico.

George learned eagerly from these vaqueros—the Mexicans' word for "cowboys"—and while he learned, he dreamed. Someday he would ride to freedom. Someday, somehow—on horseback—he would find a place for himself in the world.

There were always horses to watch and study in his father's blacksmith shop on the ranch. When they were being shod, George helped. His father taught him how to shape a metal shoe and how to nail it comfortably onto a hoof.

George's father was a proud man who hated the name the white people had given him. In addition to addressing him as "Boy," as they did all black men, they called him "Shoe Boy," because he put shoes on horses.

"Hating a name doesn't change it," he used to say. "But I aim to see the day when white folks will call me *Mr.* Shoeboy."

Even before Lincoln freed the slaves, Mr. Shoeboy had been a free man, the only one among the blacks on the ranch where John Sanders McJunkin had settled when he came from South Carolina. Mr. Shoeboy had purchased his freedom. He had bought it with money he earned working for other white ranchers after he finished all the chores Mr. McJunkin gave him to do each day.

Often Mr. Shoeboy, whose first name has been forgotten, talked about the money he was saving to buy freedom for his whole family. But work and money were scarce during the war. Ranchers didn't have many horses shod because there were no cowboys to ride them.

By June, 1865, Mr. Shoeboy still did not have enough saved up, but by that time he didn't need the money. Federal soldiers came on June 17 of that year—George never forgot the date—and told them that all blacks were free.

Never in anybody's life in Madison or Leon counties had there been a moment to equal this one. All at once people were people, not just belongings. It was a strange feeling and hard to get used to, but it was a wonderful feeling, and it made George want to cry and shout at the same time.

To George, freedom meant that he could ride whenever he wanted to, wherever he wanted to. Old Master McJunkin could not stop him from doing *anything*. His life was his own. He could choose and decide everything for himself, instead of always having to obey orders.

George was fourteen now, old enough and skilled enough to find a place in life that no slave he knew had ever been able to find before. He could be a cowboy and ride off to faraway places and learn about all kinds of wonders that slaves could not know even existed.

CHAPTER 2

Dreams of Far-Off Places

Free though he was, George did not rush to leave the place where he had grown up. For one thing, his father needed him in the blacksmith shop. Now that the war had ended, there was more work to do than there had been for years. In the early spring of 1866 the work was particularly heavy, because cowboys kept coming in, and they had many horses to be shod. They were driving large herds of longhorn cattle off to the north, and one route they followed ran past the McJunkin ranch.

George usually stole some time from the shop to take a look at the drives. Always traveling under a cloud of dust, each wide column of longhorns wound slowly across the land, writhing like a huge, single live thing. Thousands of hooves pounded the earth and made it shake. Great sweeping horns clattered and rattled against one another as heads swung in the close-packed mass. Here and there, a cow separated from her calf bawled in distress. Sometimes an epidemic of bawling swept through the whole herd.

Cowboys rode along at both sides of the herd, keeping it bunched together. Behind, still another rider watched for contrary beasts that tried to drop out and stray away.

The first cattle drives had stopped and bedded down for the night in the grassy creek bottom near Rogers Prairie. George had watched them from a distance. Then one day, when a drive approached, he went up close to have a good look.

The path he followed led through clumps of scrub oak, and he paused to gather up dead branches. Whoever was cooking for the cowboys would need firewood.

Sure enough, a campfire was already blazing. Near it stood the chuck wagon, which had traveled ahead of the cattle. A stout black man had lowered the tailgate of the wagon to form a table and was stirring something in a big iron pot.

George dropped his armload of dead branches beside the fire.

"Howdy!" said the cook. "I bet you think that little bitty wood you brought is enough to earn a full meal."

"Howdy!" George smiled. He was small for his age, and because of that, people often treated him as if he were younger than he really was. But in spite of what the cook said, George had a hunch he would be fed, even if he had come empty-handed. The fact was he liked lugging the wood. It made him feel that he was part of the whole exciting, turbulent scene.

"Try your teeth on this," the cook said and tossed George a cold biscuit left over from the night before.

"Where do you reckon they're taking all these longhorns?" George asked. It was a question that had been on his mind.

"Who wants to know?"

"Me."

"Who's me?"

"George."

The cook looked at him for a moment. "What's a banty rooster named George Something-or-other doing 'way out here?"

"I'm George from McJunkin's ranch over there."

The cook looked off beyond George, as if to say he had his doubts. There were a good many homeless black boys who had once been slaves wandering around looking for work.

"I live here. My father is a blacksmith. He's been a free man for years," he added with pride.

The cook took two iron rods from the chuck wagon and, using an ax, pounded them into the ground on either side of the fire. Then he set a crossbar on them and hung a big coffeepot over the flames.

"What about the longhorns?" George asked again.

"We're headed for the Chisholm Trail," the cook answered. "And when we get there, we'll keep on driving them north to Abilene, in Kansas."

"What for?"

"To sell 'em. Those critters are meat that is taking itself to market."

This time it was George who had his doubts. "There ain't no place where folks could eat *that* much meat!" he said.

The cook laughed. "Somebody eats it, all right. But not in Abilene. They send it to big cities in the North."

Suddenly George sensed a kind of distant rumble, the sound of a thirsty trail herd. The moment they smelled water, the longhorns—all two thousand of them—had begun to run and, swift as deer, the lanky creatures raced toward the creek. Soon the bawling, pushing, shoving mass lined the banks for half a mile, as each animal fought its neighbors for space to lower its head to the stream.

After the cattle had drunk their fill and started to graze, the cook beat on a dishpan and shouted, "Come and get it before I throw it out!"

A dozen riders—Mexican, white, and black —crowded around.

The Mexicans were like the men who worked at the ranch nearby on the San Antonio Road. George talked with them in their own language. He had learned Spanish long ago when he played with Mexican children. The white cowboys around the chuck wagon were much like those he had seen on the McJunkin ranch before the war. None of them paid any attention to him. But the blacks astonished him. For one thing, they all wore boots. More amazing, they and the Mexicans seemed to expect to eat right along with the whites.

It was first come, first served as the cook handed out big helpings of beans and biscuits, bacon, and stewed dried fruit. That was something absolutely new. Whites always got served first at the store where George went to buy candles or cornmeal for his mother.

"You can't eat beans with your fingers," the cook said to George when the cowboys had helped themselves. He held out a tin plate and a spoon.

George squatted on his bare heels, just the way the cowboys were squatting on their high-heeled boots. While the food lasted, the main sound was the rattle of spoons against plates. But afterward the men took their bedrolls from the chuck wagon, spread them out on the ground, and lay there talking.

"Reckon these critters are far enough away from their home range now so we can begin to slow down a little?" one of them said.

"Yep," said another. "They ought to be easier to handle from now on unless a thunderstorm comes up and starts them running in a stampede."

Presently a young fellow dug a violin, a fiddle, he called it, out of the chuck wagon and started a tune. Others took it up and sang. But most of the men quickly dropped off to sleep. They were bone tired. Later in the night each of them would have to get up and take his turn riding around and around the herd for two hours, keeping the cattle together. While they circled, the cowboys sang. Music, they said, calmed the longhorns.

As George walked home, the riders were already soothing the cattle:

Some of 'em go up the trails for pleasure,
But that's where they get it most awful wrong;
You ain't got any idea the trouble they give us
While we go a drivin' them all along.

The singing was quiet and faded quickly, but what George had seen around the chuck wagon stayed with him. The black cowboys were treated like people—like equals. And they rode good horses—as good as any. Not one of them had to plod along on a mule. And just like the whites, all of these men were headed for an exciting place, far away.

Back in his father's cabin, George tried to go to sleep, but he kept thinking of the black cowboys, proud in their work, guiding a dusty river of cattle to far-off places. Men who had been slaves were riding away from slave country.

Why didn't he do the same?

CHAPTER 3

Men in Masks

"I'm going to be a trail rider," George announced. But his father had other ideas.

"They got to use black riders right now," he said. "Cattle are as thick as mosquitoes in a swamp because nobody could drive them to market during the war. This summer—and maybe next—there'll be a job on trail drives for any man who can stay in the saddle. But it won't last. As soon as the extra longhorns are out of the country around here, whites will take all the regular cowboy work for themselves. Mark my word."

George listened when his father said things like that. Everybody listened to Mr. Shoeboy. They paid attention not only because he had bought his freedom and had his own shop, but also because he knew how to read. By stubbornly asking white people the meaning of words in his big Bible he managed to read it—through and through. Now George was beginning to learn, too. The verses he liked best were about bondmen in Egypt. Bondmen, he knew, were slaves, and the ones in Egypt had become free.

"We've got to read," his father said. "Otherwise we'll always be bottom rail in the fence."

"When are we going to get a school?" George asked. There had been a great deal of talk about one. When the federal troops came, they had set up a Freedmen's Bureau to help the former slaves. One thing that the Freedmen's Bureau had promised was a school.

"We'll get it soon," some people said.

But soon was a long time on the way, and Mr. Shoeboy was not hopeful.

"If the Freedmen's Bureau gets all our children to sitting down with a book," he said, "who is going to pick the white man's cotton or scare the birds out of his cornfields? You don't think Old Master is going to send his own young'uns out to do that, do you?"

Then one day, more than a year after freedom, a man came into Mr. Shoeboy's shop looking grim.

"Night riders," he said.

Everybody knew that a night rider was a white man who went about after dark, dressed in a sheet, with a mask over his face, threatening former slaves. Recently the riders had been knocking on doors around Rogers Prairie, warning black people against schools.

Masked riders even began to appear in the daytime, too, and the morning Mr. Shoeboy's friend came to the shop, he told him what had happened just the day before, on Sunday, at a little church nearby.

"When the preachin' was over," he said, "there was a row of them masked men sitting on their horses in front of the church. Didn't move. Didn't say a word."

"Didn't have to," said Mr. Shoeboy. "If we get a school, they'll burn it down the way they've been doing over toward Louisiana."

George knew that his father, who had worked hard to buy his own freedom, did not discourage easily. But now the blacksmith seemed short on hope, and George found himself feeling discouraged, too. He hated every frightening thing the night riders did. At the same time he thought more and more about the freedom he was supposed to have and about ways to get away from Rogers Prairie. The thing he wanted most was to join a trail drive. If he did go north with a herd of cattle, he might also find a chance to go to school.

What was it like in far-off Kansas where the trail drives ended? George wondered. And the more he wondered, the more his father insisted that trailing longhorns was no way for a black man to get ahead. George listened and didn't disagree—out loud. Arguing wouldn't get him what he wanted. Instead, he kept quiet and went on learning about horses.

That was easy to do because Mr. McJunkin needed help training the mounts he sold to trail drivers. He also raised mules for pulling the big freight wagons. Some of the wagons brought supplies along the San

Antonio Road from Louisiana. Others hauled buffalo hides from Indian country.

"You might just make a cowboy," Mr. McJunkin said with surprise one day when he saw George twirl a lariat in the air, then drop the loop over a fence post.

What George said in reply startled the rancher even more.

"A cowboy has to ride," George said. "Ride a horse and not a mule. Once in a while I'd like to take that old saddle you keep in the barn and throw it on a horse that isn't working."

"I reckon there'd be no harm in that," Mr. McJunkin said cautiously.

From that day on, the old saddle was on a horse a good deal more than once in a while, but George was careful not to interfere with ranch routines, and he never rode a horse too hard.

Several times a year the white cowboys who had come back to the McJunkin ranch drove herds of wild horses to the corrals. These mustangs could be used, if they could be gentled.

The cowboys fought long, hard battles with the beasts, trying to make them fit for riding. These contests fascinated George, and he watched them often, waiting for a moment that might be right for him to join in the bronc riding. At the same time he made frequent trips to the ranch down the road, where the cowboys were all Mexican. There he practiced riding untamed animals that had just come in from Indian country.

Whenever he got bucked off a horse, the vaqueros laughed good-naturedly. Then they gave practical advice.

"Shorten the stirrups. That will make it easier for you to keep your balance."

"If you get thrown, roll as you hit the ground."

"Never let a horse forget you are boss. But let him know you're pleased when he does something right."

This and more they told him in Spanish, and George understood. If only he could dress the way the vaqueros did, in a broad-brimmed hat and high-heeled boots and chaps—those leather coverings they wore on their legs for protection when they rode in thorny scrub country or broke broncs in the corral. George rode without a hat. His feet were bare, and sometimes his old wool pants got torn when he hit the ground. Nevertheless, he rode, and when he managed to stay on a bronc, the vaqueros shouted, *"Olé!"*

Before he was sixteen, George had developed a good deal of skill, and one day, when Mr. McJunkin's cowboys were tired from their struggles, George spoke up.

"I'd like to ride that buckskin bronc," he suddenly announced.

"It's your funeral," Mr. McJunkin said. "Climb aboard."

The cowboys grinned in anticipation and scrambled to the top rail of the corral to watch.

This was the chance George had been longing for. He swung a saddle up onto the bronc's back. The horse was nervous, but he let George tighten the cinch and adjust the stirrups and even put a bit in his mouth without rearing or biting or kicking. Maybe he would let George keep his seat.

George eased himself into the saddle while a cowboy held the horse's head. Then the cowboy let go.

The bronc just stood there. Gently George touched his bare heels against its sides. Then he kicked harder.

That was all it took. The bronc suddenly sprang straight up and turned in midair. He switched ends. Then he lurched up and turned again, and again. George felt as if the corral were whirling. The horse kicked his rump up high, lowered his head, and at the same moment leaned to the right. This maneuver caught George by surprise. He slid forward over the bronc's head and into the dust.

"Better stick to picking cotton, nigger boy," one of the cowboys called out, and the others laughed.

Their grating laughter sounded like the squeak of hinges—hinges on a gate to the future that was swinging shut. They would never let a black man be a cowboy if they could help it.

From that day on, George did all his bronc riding at the ranch down the road where the Mexicans worked. And he became very good at staying in the saddle on even the toughest mustang.

CHAPTER 4

Decision

By the time George was seventeen, he had made up his mind. He felt he had to move out of Rogers Prairie, where whites owned all the good land, and where they still treated blacks like slaves. He had heard that trail drives this year were forming far to the west, near a place called Comanche. He wanted to join one of the drives, but he also wanted to leave home with as little fuss as possible.

Late one afternoon in the spring of 1867, he put his blanket, his extra pants, two lariats, a small box of matches, and several chunks of corn bread into a gunnysack. He didn't try to take more food. Cowboys looking for work always got fed at any ranch where they stopped. They called it riding the chuck line.

That night, when his mother and father were asleep, George slipped out of the cabin. With his gunnysack over his shoulder, he walked along the San Antonio Road.

"Tell my folks I'm all right," he said at the first cabin he passed after sunup. "Tell them I've gone to be a cowboy—and to look for a school."

George knew that his father would not approve, and that his mother would worry and be sad. Of course, he would miss them, too. He wasn't angry with them. That wasn't why he was leaving. He just had to have more freedom to be himself than was possible in Rogers Prairie.

Before noon he did something he hadn't planned, something that surprised him. But the more he thought about it, the more he felt sure that it was right. It happened when he passed a band of McJunkin horses and an old mule that had strayed from the McJunkin place weeks before.

On an impulse, George pulled a lariat out of the gunnysack, intending to rope a horse. He would certainly rather ride than walk. And, he told himself, Old Master owed his family quite a lot for all the work they had done for him without pay when they were slaves. He had a right to take a stray horse.

On the other hand, white people would be sure to notice a black youth on a good mount, and there were stories about ugly things that had happened to men—even white men—who were regarded as horse thieves. Riding a mule would be safer than riding a horse. Blacks often did that. So George dropped a loop over the mule's head, then fashioned a lariat into a kind of halter, and scrambled onto the animal's back.

The mule would serve his purpose until he could join a trail drive. After he had a job, the boss would supply him with a horse—with many horses, in fact.

George knew that a hundred or more horses, called a remuda, accompanied every trail drive. Every morning the cowboys chose from the remuda the mounts they wanted for that day, and the wrangler took charge of the others, driving them along unsaddled. That way a man could always have a fresh horse when he needed one.

As his mule plodded along the San Antonio Road, George filled the hours with singing:

> "I wouldn't pick cotton,
> I wouldn't pitch hay,
> I wouldn't do nothin'
> That a white man say."

He also kept his eyes open for animals as he rode—deer and rabbits and armadillos. Once he tried to lasso a wild turkey. But the bird's long, thin neck slipped out of his noose, and all he caught was a flower that got tangled in his rope—a bluebonnet. Time and again he crossed whole fields turned blue by the lovely flowers.

After a while George came across one of those clownish birds that people call roadrunners. He hoped his mule would race it. He kicked her sides and switched her rump, but it was no use. She would not even break into a trot.

The roadrunner had wandered off when the mule suddenly jumped sideways, away from a sunny spot along the trail.

"Whoa, now. Slow and easy!" George stroked her neck and, looking down, saw what she had already seen—a rattlesnake, coiled and ready to strike.

Farther along, a much louder noise ripped open the hot silence of the afternoon. A combined rumble and squeak announced the approach of a freight wagon.

The driver was black. He reined in his team of four mules, obviously glad to meet someone.

"Too bad you're going the wrong way," he said. "I'm sick of talking to myself and these ornery critters. Sick of this stink, too."

His wagon held a load of hides taken from buffalo that had recently been killed on the plains. Bits of spoiled flesh clung to the hides, and they did smell awful.

"Where're you going?" the driver asked.

"I'm looking for a trail drive."

"I hear one is starting near Comanche. Just follow the wagon tracks up the Brazos, then on over to the Leon River. After a while you'll come to a corral. The road you want leaves the Leon right there. Follow it until you come to a town. Then ask."

George rode on and finally passed a few scattered cotton fields in the black earth close to the Brazos. Everything there reminded him of the plantations near the McJunkin ranch. The river made wide bends, and the wagon tracks sometimes took short-cuts, climbing over low ridges.

Before he had gone much farther, George passed a log cabin on one of the ridges. A field newly planted with corn instead of cotton came close to the cabin. Hens pecked in the yard, and some pigs lay dozing in a small pen. On the step sat a black woman pulling feathers off a freshly killed chicken.

"Come far?" she asked, and she seemed friendly.

"You heard of McJunkin's place over by the Navasota? I come from there."

"I've heard of it," the woman said. "It's a good long ways off. You must be hungry."

George smiled. He hadn't even asked her for food, and she had offered him supper. Riding the chuck line was going to be easy.

After a meal of hot corn bread and bacon, George thanked the woman and rode on to a place where she told him he'd find plenty of grass for his mule. It was still daylight when he dismounted and tied one end of his lariat to the mule's halter and the other end to a bush. That way she could eat but not wander away while George slept.

He unrolled his blanket and lay down in the sweet-smelling grass. The night was warm. No need to use any of his precious matches to make a fire. He just lay on his back and looked up at the stars. From nearby came the swishing sound of water in the river. Far away he heard dogs barking, and once he heard a coyote howl.

At first the night was dark, except for the stars. Then the moon rose and lit up the meadow. George lay especially quiet when he saw the black and white stripes of a mother skunk, followed by five youngsters, waddling down toward the edge of the water.

An owl hooted, and hooted again. Once in a while a mockingbird seemed to be singing in its sleep.

George had thought he would feel very much alone this first night by himself. But aloneness wasn't what he felt so much as excitement. He was in a new place—in a new night, and the night was full of wonder. He was on the road to living a new life—his own life.

Next day George met more freighters, some black and some white. All of them were hauling smelly loads of buffalo hides, and two also had supplies of dried buffalo meat. Jerky, they called it. They were glad to give George strips of the tough stuff, which was hard to chew but tasted good, and it kept him from being hungry.

Finally George turned away from the Brazos and headed for the Leon. Here and there along the wagon tracks, a solitary man, or a man and his wife, had cut chunks of sod out of the prairie and piled them up, brick-fashion, to form the walls of a house. The people who lived in these soddies fed him, too. One of them even paid him to help dig a well. When the job was done, George wrapped a strip of cloth around a fistful of quarters that the man had given him. It was the first money he had ever earned, and he wanted to take good care of it.

A little cluster of houses made up the town of Comanche, the place that the freighter had told him about. "Anybody around here looking for cowboys?" George asked a man on the street. The man was white. There were no blacks anywhere.

"There's a trail herd forming west of town," the man told him. "But I doubt if they will take you on."

"They won't hire blacks," George thought. Then he had another idea. Maybe they just didn't hire blacks who were barefoot. The man was looking at George's feet.

Boots and just about everything else were for sale at a store in town. George tied his mule to a post at the back of the store where he knew blacks would have to go.

The boots he got felt strange. Until now he had always gone barefoot, and he walked clumsily in the secondhand pair that his handful of quarters had bought. Men lounging against the building stared at him with hard eyes as he went down the street. He was glad to get out of Comanche.

CHAPTER 5

Trailing Longhorns

"Did you come through Comanche?" the trail boss asked.

George nodded.

"You got guts. The other day they strung up a nigger kid there. He was just about your age."

George gasped. For a moment he felt as if his own breath was being choked out.

"I like guts," the boss went on. "And I need a wrangler. You're hired."

George hesitated. He hadn't been trying to be brave, for he didn't know about the killing. So he was getting credit he didn't deserve. At the same time, he was being offered a less important job than he had hoped for. He had dreamed of being a regular cowboy, not just a wrangler, who had to work harder and got paid less than real cowboys. Still, the job would take him away from the hateful Texas world, which still surrounded him, even here at the edge of Indian country. The wrangler was the cook's helper as well as the one who took care of the horses that trail drivers rode. At least the experience might help him to get cowboy work later on.

And so George turned his mule loose on the prairie and before dawn the next day the cook called him to start the fire for coffee.

Every day, after that, George drove the remuda, sometimes ahead of the cattle, sometimes well off to one side. But if he got a late start, he had to follow along behind the herd in clouds of dust so thick he couldn't breathe unless he covered his nose and mouth with his bandanna.

When he could see through the dust, he was fascinated by a trick the dragman had. This cowboy, whose job it was to keep the cattle from lagging behind or straying, had made his lariat into a whip. With the loop end in his hand, he snapped out the other end and flicked the backs of the animals that weren't keeping up. Leather strips attached to the end of the lariat cracked like a shot each time. George soon learned the trick, and he spent a lot of time snapping his rope.

Every morning the chuck wagon went out ahead of the herd and stopped near some grassy place before noon. Then the cook, with George helping, prepared the big meal of the day. Often he stewed potatoes and some fresh-killed beef and made sourdough biscuits in iron pots called Dutch ovens. Usually he served coffee, sweetened with molasses, and stewed dried fruit or a rice-and-raisin pudding that the men called spotted pup.

The nooning—the midday stop—was a time of rest for cowboys and cattle and horses, but not for George. He had to wash the tin plates and cups, which the cowboys had thrown into what they called the wreck pan. At the same time he had to keep an eye on the remuda to make sure the horses did not wander off too far. At the end of the long day he helped the cook prepare son-of-a-gun stew, a concoction of all the leftovers from the midday meal plus anything else the cook felt like throwing into the pot. Then came more dishwashing. When he crawled into his bedroll at last, it was usually well after dark. If he wasn't too tired to think about it, he was glad then that he would not have to get up in the middle of the night to take a turn riding around the herd the way the other hands did.

"How do you know when your turn is over?" he asked a waddy one evening.

The cowboy pointed to the eastern horizon and the stars just above it. Different stars, he said, would be showing there in two hours, still others in another two hours, and so on through the night.

Once in a while George woke up when he heard the riders changing the watch, and he got into the habit of looking with one sleepy eye to see what stars were showing in the low edge of the sky to the east. At other times he also noticed where the handle of the Big Dipper was pointing. That was another way of telling time at night. Sometimes the night sky made him feel he was on the edge of a world countless times larger than the one he already knew.

This stargazing habit George got into on the trail drive would stay with him for the rest of his life. In time his wonderment about planets and constellations and the Milky Way would link up with curiosity about other things in the natural world. But at the moment his interest was purely practical.

Then one night when he threw his bedroll on the ground, not a star was in sight. Clouds covered the sky.

"Looks like a storm," the trail boss said to George. "Keep a horse saddled. If the cattle get spooked, we'll need you to help."

Later a clap of thunder woke George. At the same time rain started to fall—and the ground began to shake.

"Stampede!" the cook shouted to George. "Ride with the herd. We'll try to get it circling."

George was on his feet in an instant, his heart pounding with excitement—and fear. The night was so dark that he had to feel for the stirrup before he could swing into the saddle and turn toward the thundering hooves. His horse seemed to see well enough, however, even to enjoy racing the swift-footed longhorns, which had been frightened by the storm. A sudden flash of lightning revealed the herd. Two cowboys were forcing cattle toward the left, so George swung his rope and yelled and urged his horse in that direction.

Gradually the frenzied creatures began to wheel in a great circle. The riders had succeeded in driving

the head of the herd around until it joined the tail.
Now the danger was over. Most of the herd, at least,
had been kept together, and the cattle would not run
off the edge of some bluff and kill themselves.
George relaxed in the dark and patted his horse's
neck, enjoying the feel of the animal's thumping
heart against his legs.

When George had been on the trail for more than
two months, he began to get tired of the monotonous
work and to long for the new things he was bound to
find in Dodge City. His tight-curled hair was very
shaggy by now, so he asked the cook to give him a
haircut. All the other men did the same. But everyone had to shave himself.

"I'd rather cut your throats than your whiskers,"
the cook said cheerfully.

When the cattle were all bedded down outside
Dodge City, the boss hired some night herders and
paid off his crew. With money in their pockets,
George and the other cowboys spurred their horses
and galloped toward town.

At the edge of the scrawny village the horses suddenly took fright, and George could hardly blame
them. A railroad locomotive, the first he had ever
seen, loomed monstrous on a track. Its great pound-
ing wheels and bellowing engine shook the ground.
Behind it rolled cars filled with bawling cattle.

George pulled his horse up short. The whole huge
mechanical marvel fascinated him. A man was shoveling coal onto a blazing fire inside the locomotive.
Another leaned out of the engine's window, while

still another ran nimbly along the tops of the cattle cars. Just the sight of the train was worth the two long months on the trail. And there was still the town to see.

With a mixture of hope and misgiving George had been trying to imagine what Dodge City would be like. The only other town he had ever seen was Comanche, and what had happened there did not reassure him.

It took very little time to size up Dodge. The first man to be locked up in the new jail was black. At the cafés, he was told, "No niggers allowed." Clearly, the freedom George sought was somewhere else—if it was anywhere.

After one trip to town, George took his meals at his own outfit's chuck wagon. His money went for a new hat and new pants, an old saddle, and a fair horse. Then he had to decide what to do. Should he follow other black cowboys farther north? It was almost the end of summer, when work always grew scarce. Perhaps he might not find any job at all if he went north.

The trail boss settled the problem. "Do you want to ride for me again next spring?" he asked George.

"Wrangling horses?"

"Punching cattle," the boss said, and he gave George a friendly slap on the shoulder. That meant he was offering him work as a regular cowboy, not just as a wrangler.

So George turned back south on the same trail he had just covered, and he traveled alone.

When he came near Comanche again, he made a wide swing around the town. In a draw a few miles beyond, he came on a band of horses so scrawny-looking that nobody would bother to claim them. With them was a mule George recognized—the one he had ridden away from the McJunkin ranch many months before. On impulse he dropped a loop over its head and made a rope halter for it.

Leading the mule slowed him down, but time was something he could spare, and when he finally turned the animal loose in one of Mr. McJunkin's pastures, George felt good. He had found a way to say that he could get along very well now by himself. He did not need any help—not even a mule—from John Sanders McJunkin, who owed him plenty.

At the blacksmith shop his father greeted him warmly. Then his manner changed a little. He stood back and studied George. "You know what people say? Up the river they say that just about the time you left a young fellow rode through on one of Mr. McJunkin's mules."

"People say that?" George laughed. "People'll say anything. I just saw a worthless old mule that might be the one you mean. She's out there in the south pasture."

CHAPTER 6

What's Your Name?

George paid his family a long visit. Now, whenever he spoke of being a cowboy, his father raised no objections. It seemed as if the old man thought: A blacksmith is held to his shop like a bull tied with a ring in his nose. But a cowboy on a horse is free to move. He can ride on when troubles get too big to handle.

Troubles there were. A white preacher had come to Rogers Prairie, talking up the school idea. The next morning they found a picture of a coffin carved on the door of the cabin where he stayed. If he didn't leave, the night riders said, his next sermon would be preached in hell.

George was already thinking of the trail. Early in the spring of 1868, when the land first became a mass of bluebonnets, he said good-bye to his parents and rode off toward Comanche for the job the trail boss had promised him.

Partway up the Brazos River he came upon an outfit the likes of which he had never seen before. Two white men and a youth about his own age rode beneath a cloud of dust raised by hundreds of hooves, but the hooves belonged to horses, not longhorns. The usual wagon accompanied the riders, but its driver was a woman. On the seat beside her sat two small children. A baby slept in her lap.

The white boy hailed George and struck up a conversation. Jabe was his name, he said, Jabe Burton. When his folks died he'd been sort of adopted by Gideon Roberds, the older of the two men. The other was Gideon's brother. The woman was Gideon's wife Jane.

For a while George rode alongside Jabe, who seemed glad to have company. Near sundown the little party stopped, and all the men dismounted—except George. Was he welcome to stay with them for the night?

Before he could decide, Jabe's horse snorted, then raced off across the plain. Without thinking, George did what he had done many a time on the trail drive when a cowboy's horse took fright at a snake or an insect sting or some nameless sudden motion. He spurred his own horse and lit out after it.

In moments he had his lariat up under a hind foot of the frightened runaway. The rope, turned around his saddle horn, slowed the horse. Soon George could grab its reins and lead it back to Jabe.

Gideon Roberds had seen this quick display of skill. "Where'd you learn to handle a rope?" he asked, showing real surprise.

"I was raised on a horse ranch."

"Ever ride a bronc?"

"Breaking horses was the main thing on the ranch," George said, and his answer tickled him. He was discovering the delight of saying one thing when he meant something quite different. Let the white man guess the truth. No use saying outright that he hadn't done any of Mr. McJunkin's bronc busting—that he had gone to the Mexican ranch to practice that art.

Gideon Roberds looked skeptical, and so did his brother.

"You got a bronc you want ridden?" George asked quietly.

"Jabe, help him throw a saddle on that big gray we picked up yesterday," Gideon ordered.

Then, before he fully realized what was happening, George was up in the saddle and off on a ride that would change the course of his life.

The gray was a wily opponent. George had to use all his skill to stay aboard, but he managed, and in time the horse, tired out, stopped its lunges and jumps and turns.

Gideon Roberds watched the ride with growing interest. When George pulled the saddle off the quivering animal and sent him back into the herd, Gideon said, "How would you like to come along with my outfit and help get some of these knotheads ready to sell?"

The unexpected question left George without words. A year ago he had never worked for pay. Now he had to choose between two jobs. He could go on and join the trail drive that was forming somewhere near Comanche. Or he could stay and train horses.

Work with horses interested him a good deal more than herding cattle. With horses there was always something new and different and exciting. You could see them learn and change. You couldn't teach a longhorn much of anything, and the same old tasks went on day after day. But what kind of man was Gideon Roberds? What would he be like to work for?

"Well?" said Gideon.

"I—I don't know." George needed some time to think. This white man didn't seem to know as much about the country, or even about horses, as George's old trail boss did. He wore fancier clothes than Mr. McJunkin had ever worn except on Sunday, and Mrs. Roberds didn't swear and chew snuff the way some of the white women back in Rogers Prairie did. She offered him supper, and he thanked her. But when it came time to eat, it was plain that the whole Roberds family expected George to take his plate off by himself.

"What do you say?" Gideon asked after the meal was over. "Do you want a job?"

"I've already got a job," George said. "I'm going to Comanche to join a trail drive."

"I'll pay better money than you can get on a trail drive. It will be steady work, too. All year round, if you turn out to be really good with horses. This will be the first horse outfit in these parts, and I'm going to move it on farther west. We'll be selling riding stock to trail bosses. There'll be a market for all kinds of horses along the Santa Fe Trail, too."

George could feel Gideon's enthusiasm. Clearly this white man had big plans. Working for him might be a chance he would never get again.

"I'll make up my mind by morning," George said.

From Jabe Burton he learned that Gideon Roberds had been a planter in Georgia.

"He had a whole pack of slaves," said Jabe.

George looked up. The white boy was boasting, but at the same time he didn't seem the least bit hostile. Could it be that he had so little to boast about that he grabbed on to something like this in an effort to feel important?

But the information that Gideon Roberds had been a slave owner gave George a new reason to be cautious. The boss on the trail drive had never owned slaves, and he had treated George just the way he treated the white cowboys. Would it be a step backward, away from freedom, to join up with Gideon Roberds?

The decision George had to make was hard, but as he unrolled his blanket for the night, he knew that his mind was made up. The horses grazing nearby had helped him decide. His future had to be with them, not with longhorns. And as for Gideon Roberds, George felt about him the way he did when he swung up into the saddle on a strange bronc. He didn't know what was going to happen, but he was determined to stay aboard.

A feeling of excitement, mixed with a kind of calm, spread through George as he lay on his back looking up at the stars. Was this the way it felt to be a man—a free, grown man?

"I'll come along," George told Gideon next morning.

"Then I'd better find out what to call you," Roberds said.

"They call me George."

"Just George? Didn't the Northerns give you any other name when they came through after the war?"

The federal soldiers had not given him any other name. Neither had the people in the Freedmen's Bureau. When he went on the trail drive, no one had cared if he had more than one name. He was just George.

"What did they call your pappy?" Roberds persisted.

George hesitated. He had always hated the name Shoeboy.

"I'm George from McJunkin's place," he mumbled, and hoped the answer would do.

"All right, then—George McJunkin."

George said nothing, but a little of the feeling he had had the night before was gone—the feeling of being a man, his own man. Now, like many another black, he was to go through the rest of his life as if he still belonged in some way to the man who had once owned him.

This naming took place in Texas, on the prairie, where grazing land seemed endless. But Gideon

Roberds did not intend to stay there. He was sure he would find a good market for horses farther west. Cattlemen already talked about trailing herds north through New Mexico, and that was where the Santa Fe Trail ended. So, moving slowly from one water hole to another, the Roberds brothers and George and Jabe Burton shifted the herd north and west onto the Staked Plain.

It was risky, the dream that Gideon Roberds had of driving his mustangs to market across the great Staked Plain. This was Comanche Indian country, and Comanches often stole horses from whites who, in turn, were busy stealing the Indians' land.

CHAPTER 7

Horse Stealing

George reined in his horse and stared. A chasm opened before him in the almost flat surface of the Staked Plain. So this was Palo Duro Canyon! The walls went almost straight down, but a band of green at the bottom meant water and grass for the horses.

A steep trail, probably made by buffalo, led into the canyon. It wasn't easy for George and Jabe and Gideon's brother to get seven hundred horses single file down that trail. But they managed. Meanwhile, Gideon rode beside the wagon that his wife Jane was driving. They found, as they had hoped, an easier way into the canyon and made rendezvous with the others later.

A stream trickled along the canyon floor, even in late September, a dry time of year. There was still plenty of grass, although small bands of buffalo were grazing in a few places. Next morning Gideon looked at the water and the grass and the high, sheltering rock walls, and he decided to winter there.

George went to work cutting down trees and help-ing to put up a log cabin for Gideon and his family. Then he helped to build a log fence around a small pasture for the riding horses and a corral they could use for gentling some of the mustangs. Finally George and Jabe built a small log shelter for them-selves. They slept there, and that was where George ate.

Eating by himself, away from the whites, was part of the slave world George had hoped to leave be-hind. But at least he was far from the actual land where blacks had been nothing but work animals, no better than mules.

Although Palo Duro Canyon was far inside Indian country, George did not find any fresh signs of In-dians as he rode, sometimes upstream and sometimes down, checking for horses that might be straying off. He did see buffalo aplenty, and for months buffalo meat was the main source of food for the day party.

All went quietly in the deep canyon until one day when Gideon and his brother and Jabe rode up onto the open plain to look for stray horses they could round up and add to the herd. George had stayed behind to gather firewood about a half mile from the cabin. Suddenly, while he was working in a sparse grove of saplings, he heard a rumble in the earth. It made him tense up with memories of stampedes on the trail drive. The thunder sound rolled closer. Soon enough he knew it was made by hundreds of pound-ing hooves—the hooves of horses running at full speed.

The first of the Roberds herd raced past, heads high, manes flying. George's own mount, terrified and caught up in the frenzy of the stampede, broke free from the sapling to which he had been tied. He dashed off and joined the speeding herd, taking with him not only the saddle on his back, but also George's rifle, which had been attached to it.

Like a flash flood the horses poured by, and George could only watch the sudden torrent of frightened creatures. Then he saw what had spooked them, and he felt panic of a kind he had never known before. He could only stand and stare, as unable to move as the scatter of trees around him.

Half a dozen Indians, yelling and waving rifles, were driving the herd down the canyon. Suddenly two of them saw George and swerved toward him. Guiding their mounts skillfully with their knees while they held their rifles ready to fire, the Indians came straight on. But when they saw that George was unarmed, they dropped their weapons to their laps and slowed to a trot.

"Black Mexican can walk now," one of them said and laughed.

By "Black Mexican" he obviously meant George. The other Indian, who seemed to speak no English, said something to his companion. George was sure the words meant that they ought to shoot him and waste no more time.

The English-speaking Indian appeared to disagree, perhaps because now some of the horses at the rear of the herd were slowing down.

Too quickly to believe, the rifles that had been threatening George's life now waved at the horses. The Indians raced off, not even bothering to look back at him.

A long moment passed before George knew he was safe, at least for the time being. Death, which had come up to him and frozen him with fear, had gone on past.

As soon as he could begin to think clearly, he realized with new horror that the Indians would be passing the cabin just about now. Mrs. Roberds didn't have a rifle. She had suggested that morning that George take hers with him.

"You might see a deer or a turkey," she said.

Fear for Mrs. Roberds and the children set George's legs to moving. He didn't know what he could do, but he had to reach the cabin as fast as possible.

Not an Indian or a horse was in sight as he ran, panting, up to the door. Mrs. Roberds stood there, pale and speechless, holding little Coke, the baby, in her arms.

"You all right?" George gasped.

She nodded and knelt to put an arm around the two children, Mattie and Emmett, who had been holding tight to her skirt.

"Look," she finally managed to say, "they're all gone, every one of them." Her eyes swept the pasture, where horses had been grazing quietly a few minutes before.

Not one was left anywhere near the cabin or, for

that matter, anywhere in the canyon. The Indians had run off the whole herd that Gideon Roberds had assembled, except—George hoped—the three that Gideon and his brother and Jabe were riding.

All that day, George and Jane Roberds worked to pile up logs in front of the cabin door and window, in case the Indians decided to come back. George had no weapon with which to fight off an attack, but the log barriers might slow the Indians and give Gideon time enough to come to the rescue.

No Indians appeared. Apparently they had watched the Roberds party carefully and made a daylight raid because they knew that three of the four men were away. They were not interested in harming Mrs. Roberds or the children or George. All they wanted was horses.

When the three men returned a few days later, driving a dozen mustangs they had rounded up, they were aghast and angry at the clean sweep the Indians had made.

"What did six Indians want with all those horses?" George asked Jabe that night when they settled down in the log shelter. "They couldn't use all seven hundred of them."

"They were Comanches," Jabe replied. "Don't you know why Comanches steal horses? They steal to show that they're tough hombres. Everybody is going to look up to those six warriors when they get back to their camp, wherever it is. A Comanche gets a lot of respect if he can steal horses from the enemy. But he never steals from another Comanche.

In a way, horse stealing is a game. And they sure enough won a great big game against Gideon."

But to Gideon Roberds, horse stealing was in no sense a game. He himself took horses where he found them, and he planned to sell them. That was his way of making money. On the other hand, the Comanches took very little interest in wealth. It was adventure and prestige that they wanted. A man with many horses was admired, particularly if he had obtained them with daring and with gaiety.

Gideon seemed to feel that he as a white man was the only one who had a right to round up the animals. And he began at once to put together a new herd. Every day he and his brother and Jabe rode onto the open plain. Often they returned to the canyon driving a few horses ahead of them. During these expeditions George stayed at the cabin with a rifle he hoped he wouldn't have to use.

By spring Gideon had a herd nearly as large as the one he had brought into the canyon. Some of the animals had been branded, so no doubt they had escaped from settlers on the edge of Indian country. Others were the wild descendants of horses brought into the area centuries before by the Spaniards. It didn't matter to Gideon whether they were wild or just strays that already bore brands. He placed his own brand, the numeral 30, on the left shoulder of every horse he found.

A surprising number of the animals were from his original herd. Why they now ran loose on the plains was a mystery. George didn't learn until much later

that the United States Army was giving the Comanches so much trouble that they had no time to
protect the horses they had assembled. Indeed, the
army had almost completed its victory over them.

Only twice after the stampede did the party in the
canyon see evidence that Indians were still
around—at least a few of them. One day Gideon and
his brother surprised a young fellow who had apparently been hunting. Without a moment's hesitation,
the Roberds brothers fired. The youth dropped dead.

When Gideon came back to the cabin, he ordered
George to bury the body.

"It won't be healthy for us if the Comanches come
across that corpse," he said.

George rode off to do a job that he hated.

When the herd of horses in Palo Duro Canyon was
back to its former size, Gideon and his brother relaxed a little. One day they went hunting for turkeys,
which would be a change from their steady diet of
buffalo meat.

Some distance from the cabin they sighted a number of the birds scattered over a wide area. The two
men separated to make sure they would kill as many
as possible. Gideon's brother was soon out of sight
behind a small hill. When he did not reappear, Gideon followed around the hill, and there he saw
what had happened.

His brother lay dead, killed by a silent ax. How
long had an Indian been waiting for a moment when
one of the Roberds brothers would be off guard? No
matter. He had found a way of getting revenge for

the death of the young hunter the white men had shot.

Gideon now lost no time in leaving Palo Duro Canyon. He gave the horses little rest until they reached good grazing land in what is now the eastern part of New Mexico.

George was glad when they seemed to be out of Indian country. He had no quarrel with the Comanches and no desire to risk his life in a fight with those dark riders who stole gaily and for honor, instead of grimly and for greed, as white men seemed to do.

CHAPTER 8

The Cimarron

Gideon Roberds grazed his horses a long time in New Mexico. While he tarried, George gentled the wild animals, readying them for sale. Sometimes he also rode out over the country looking for strays. On one of these rides he picked up an object that he kept with him in all his later travels, an object that had meaning for him for the rest of his life.

A recent rainstorm had washed away some earth and made a new channel near the creek. In the side of this arroyo George saw some bones sticking out of the ground. They weren't buffalo bones. He knew that, because he had seen thousands of buffalo skeletons scattered over the Staked Plain where hunters had left them, and he'd butchered a good many buffalo himself.

George got off his horse and took a closer look. With his knife he dug earth away from one piece of bone that scarcely showed. In a moment the whole thing came out in his hand. A human skull! Suddenly he remembered the Comanche he had had to bury. He shivered a little, but he dug farther and found some gray stone beads and a stone ax.

Once, he thought, there had been a face on that skull, and life inside it. The face and bones and life had belonged to an Indian. No one but Indians would have buried their dead with stone beads and a stone ax—and in this lonely spot. Was it the grave of a Comanche, perhaps an ancestor of the raiders he had encountered in the canyon? George had no interest in meeting any more such men. With the skull in his hand, he wanted even more to avoid them, for fear of what they might do if they found he had it. At the same time, he couldn't think of giving it up. He was curious about it, as he was curious about many things.

George hid the skull in a bag of beans that rested on the floor of the chuck wagon. If Comanches did visit the camp, they would not be likely to find it there.

As it happened, the Roberds party met no more Indians. They met nobody at all until they shifted the herd to a beautiful valley that ran along the base of an enormous ridge, which has since come to be known as Johnson Mesa. At first the only people George saw were a few Mexicans tending flocks of sheep or herds of cattle.

The Mexicans called the river there the Cimarron Seco, the Dry Cimarron, because it sometimes dried up. The name Cimarron had a meaning that appealed to George. It was a name the Mexicans gave to an animal that had run away and gone wild, and in this country there were many such wild horses and cattle and sheep. That wasn't all. Back in Texas, George had heard the word *cimarron* used for a slave who had struck out for freedom—who had run away, gone wild.

Altogether the valley of the Dry Cimarron seemed to be the kind of place he would like. The more he rode up and down the river, looking for horses, the more he thought this place was right for him.

The valley looked especially rich and lovely from the top of a high, cone-shaped mountain that George climbed one day. Capulin Mountain, the Mexicans called it, because *capulin* was their word for the chokecherry bushes that covered its sides. The rocks under the bushes seemed very strange; they were different from any George had ever seen. They were jagged, and their edges cut into his boots when he got off his horse to walk. He picked up a small piece of the rock and put it in his pocket, and for a long time he wondered about it. Years later he found out that it had once spilled, hot and glowing, from inside the earth when Capulin Mountain was a live volcano.

Looking out north from the mountaintop, George could see for miles along the Dry Cimarron valley, and it reminded him of a Bible story his father had read to him. When slaves escaped from Egypt, the Bible said, they had been promised a land of their own, a place that was full of "hills and valleys and drinketh water of the rain of heaven." Just now, over on Johnson Mesa, a shower was falling. The Promised Land must have been very much like the valley of the Dry Cimarron.

In a way the oak thickets around the valley also reminded George of the thickets on the low hills around Rogers Prairie. This place was very much like his first home, except that here no men had grown used to having slaves do their work for them. Here, he thought, he and more of his people could live happily.

On his way down the mountain, George came to a little camp where a Mexican watched a herd of sheep. The man's name was Tony Cornay, and he offered George food and good talk. George spoke to him in Spanish, and the two soon became friends.

Later George met other Mexicans, among them Candido Archuletta. Candido was a cattleman. Usually his longhorns grazed in the grassy open country, but they also liked to hide among thick growths of scrubby trees. Then there was trouble. The cattle could dodge into the dense clumps, where a man on horseback couldn't follow them. It took hard, patient work to get them out. Candido was not especially patient, and he solved the problem with a clever invention. He cut thin bars of strong wood and fastened them to the tips of the long horns, so that the bars stretched across the animals' foreheads. Wearing one of these devices, even the smartest old cow found it hard to slip in among the trees. Most of the cattle learned to stay out in the open.

One day, Candido and George met strangers in the

valley. A caravan of covered wagons, with perhaps a hundred people in all, had camped on the Dry Cimarron. They were the thinnest, palest, sorriest lot George had ever seen. Not one of them knew a thing about living on the frontier. They had come from cities in the East looking for work—any kind of work—because they couldn't find jobs at home. Thousands of able-bodied men were unemployed everywhere, they said.

How could there be half-starved men, women, and children in a country full of meat? Candido wasted no time wondering. He butchered two of his steers to feed the people in the caravan. Then he gave them two more that they could drive along and kill later. The Archulettas were like that.

As George rode around keeping track of the Roberds horses or going on visits from one new friend to another, he carried Gideon's rifle in a scabbard on the right side of his saddle. Sometimes he used it to bring down a deer or an antelope. Once he shot a bear that was digging something out of a hollow oak tree. What the bear had found was honey. George came back later and got several bucketfuls of it—and a few beestings, too.

Along the river the meadows, which the Mexicans called vegas, turned blue with wild iris blossoms in the springtime. The sight made George think of the bluebonnets in Texas, but somehow it didn't make him homesick. This new country had become home.

Up the river lived an English-speaking sheepman named Mingus. He and his wife were lonely and glad for George's company. Mrs. Mingus, George discovered, liked to help him read from the Bible. Some of the verses reminded him of what he had heard about cattle roundups. "Thou shalt not see thy brother's ox or his sheep go astray . . . thou shalt in any case bring them again unto thy brother."

With its sheep and cattle the Dry Cimarron was a beautiful place, but its people were few, and they seldom bought horses. Not many travelers followed the Cimarron Cut-off, a shortcut from the Santa Fe Trail that crossed the valley. Most traffic bound for Santa Fe used the main trail farther north. In addition, the men who drove longhorns across the valley already had large remudas.

Many of the cattle drives followed a route laid out by a man named Charles Goodnight, who brought his herds past Capulin Mountain and down to the rich grass in the vegas. Then, when his animals were strong and rested, he drove them up over Johnson Mesa and on north. This practice gave Gideon Roberds an idea. If it paid Goodnight to cross the mesa, it might pay Gideon to do the same. There might be a better market for horses near the town of Trinidad, which was forty or fifty miles away to the northwest, directly on the main trail to Santa Fe. So Gideon told George and Jabe Burton to take his herd over the mesa.

Always before, when Roberds decided to move on, George had been eager to see what lay ahead. This time he thought only of the good things he would be leaving behind. Besides, Candido Archuletta had told him grim, disturbing stories about Trinidad.

A few years ago, Candido said, a real war had broken out there between the Mexicans and the Anglos—that is, the English-speaking whites. The fighting started at a Christmas celebration. As part of the festivities, a Mexican and an Anglo had a wrestling match. The Mexican won. That irritated the Anglos, and they started to shoot. The Mexicans shot back. Soon about five hundred Mexicans and five hundred Anglos were firing at each other whenever they got a chance. Finally the Anglos, with the help of soldiers, won the war, and most of the fighting stopped. But the town stayed full of hate.

Nevertheless, George took the herd over the mesa for Roberds. East of Trinidad, on the Picketwire River, Gideon chose a place for a ranch, and George settled down to a steady routine of exciting work. While Gideon and Jabe put up cabins and corrals and a schoolhouse, George turned his skill with horses into more and more of an art.

As fast as the well-gentled mounts were sold, Gideon added new stock to his herd, and so George kept busy year after year. Along with training horses, he began to train boys. When Gideon's sons, Emmett and Coke, were old enough, George taught them to ride and to rope. But he demanded a price for his tutoring. He exchanged riding lessons for reading lessons. After Emmett and Coke finished their day in the schoolhouse their father had built, George borrowed their textbooks, and he got the boys to help him puzzle out the words he didn't know.

"No reading, no riding," he said whenever the boys wanted to skip their half of the bargain.

That was during the day. In the evening George often rode off to one of the Mexican communities, called plazas. There were several plazas within a two-hour ride of the Roberds ranch, each made up of half a dozen little brown adobe houses. In front of each house sat a dome-shaped adobe oven, in which the women baked a bread that was different from the kind George got on the ranch. He liked it, and he liked the highly spiced foods the women cooked indoors over fires in small fireplaces built in corners of the rooms.

Mexican houses were filled with color and a gaiety that George loved. Strings of bright red or green peppers hung on the white walls, along with colored pictures of saints. When the weather was cold, the people held dances in one house or another. In good weather they celebrated outdoors. And indoors or out they sang and played guitars.

George watched the musicians' quick fingers. Presently, with a little help, he learned how to play, too. The next time he went to Trinidad for ranch supplies, he bought a guitar. On another trip he spent his wages on a violin. Still later he bought a good hunting rifle.

Now he often played the guitar when he visited his Mexican friends in the plazas. He also fiddled for dances at the Anglo ranches that were springing up along the Picketwire. And wherever he went, he would take along a gift of meat from a deer or an antelope he had shot with his own new rifle.

When he didn't go visiting at night, George studied. With the help of Emmett and Coke, he learned to write as well as read, and together they finished all the school books through the fourth grade.

Both boys worked along with George as he trained the horses that bore Gideon's "30" brand. This brand was becoming famous up and down the Picketwire. Everyone knew that the Roberds ranch was the place to go if you wanted a horse that could start quickly and turn fast. Properly trained, such an animal became a cutting horse. It could go in among a herd of cattle and help the rider cut—that is, separate—a calf from its mother, then drive it off to be branded. Ranchers paid good prices for the cutting horses that George trained. He was well known and respected for his very special skills. He had begun to make a place for himself in the world.

Life on the Roberds ranch was busy, but George had time to make friends—even in Trinidad. When he had to drive the ranch wagon into town to buy supplies, he often put his team in the livery stable for safekeeping. There he met Gene Ferguson, the man who worked in the stable.

"You're about the only Anglo in town who doesn't think that black and bad mean the same thing," George said one night as they shared a meal in Gene's adobe house.

"You're the only man here who talks English who doesn't try to reform me or rob me," Gene replied.

Robbers did hang out in Trinidad. For a while the town hired the frontier lawman Bat Masterson to deal with some of the outlaws. According to one story, Billy the Kid, the most famous of all Western desperadoes, rode into town one day and announced that he was going to kill the doctors who lived there—all four of them. Nobody remembers why he had a grudge against doctors, but years later a Catholic nun wrote the story of how she had talked Billy the Kid out of committing these murders.

Every man in Trinidad carried a gun. So did every rancher and cowboy for hundreds of miles around, particularly in No Man's Land, as the westernmost part of Oklahoma was called.

One day a representative of the 101 Ranch, close to No Man's Land, came to the Roberds place and asked George if he would help with the roundup. George was glad to oblige a neighbor, even a distant one. And besides, the roundup would be a change.

At the 101, George met two young white cowboys who used their guns in a crazy daredevil game, trying to see how close they could come to killing each other without actually drawing blood. When these two got into a shooting mood, they would fire at each other from behind separate log cabins. The bullets they used gave off little puffs of black smoke, so that the one being shot at could see the smoke before the bullet actually reached him. If he kept his eyes open, and if he dodged in time, he would not get hit. Of course, if he failed to see the telltale smoke, or if the other fellow aimed too close, it might be his last shoot-out.

Life, it seemed to George, was not something to be wasted in this idiotic way. Since he was a better shot than either of the cowboys, he soon figured out a way to break up their game and have a little fun into the bargain. The next time they got ready for a shoot-out, George loaded his own gun with smokeless bullets. Then he hid in a place where he could see both of them but where neither of them would notice him.

When the first cowboy fired, George instantly fired at him, aiming at the wall above his head. The bullet knocked splinters off a log, and the cowboy ducked. What was going on? He could see no smoke from the log cabin behind which his opponent was hiding—or anywhere else.

The second fellow fired, and George put a bullet in the wall just above *his* head. Now *he* was mystified—and scared. How could the bullet travel so fast that he couldn't see smoke before it hit?

It didn't take long for the two cowboys to decide that their game was getting too rough. The shooting stopped. George kept his joke to himself, and the young fellows didn't know until much later that he had tricked them and how he had done it.

Around this time some of the 101 cowboys became curious about a little box that George kept in the bunkhouse. They wanted to know what was in it, but they couldn't find out. The trouble was that the box lid would open only at the touch of a secret spring. When George wasn't around, they experimented and finally pushed the spring. The lid flew

open. Inside the box lay a collection of rock specimens, fossils, and crystals that George had found
and saved. The boys poked around looking for something more interesting than rocks, but found nothing.

That night George discovered the mix-up in the
box. He didn't say a word, but anyone who knew
him could have guessed he was working out a
scheme. Later, when the others were not around, he
stuffed the box with light, fluffy feathers from a duck
he had shot and put it back in its usual place.

Again curiosity got the better of some cowboy.
This time George didn't have to look inside to know
that the box had been opened. Tiny downy feathers
lay scattered all over the bunkhouse floor.

When George came in he picked up a bit of the
down and studied it very solemnly.

"Seems like you sometimes find duck feathers in
funny places," he said, and he let the down float
back to the floor.

Nobody meddled with his box again.

After the 101 roundup ended, Ben Smith, the
ranch foreman, asked George an important question.
"How would you like to have a regular job working
for Dr. Owen?" he said.

Dr. Owen was one of the partners who owned the
101. He had other property just over the mountains
in New Mexico, and he had been the first mayor of
Trinidad.

"The doctor's starting up a new place," Ben Smith
went on. "I thought maybe you'd like to give him a
hand with his thoroughbreds."

George knew that Dr. Owen kept the finest horses anywhere in that part of the West. The idea of working with such superb animals was very tempting. Moreover, the doctor's new place was in the valley of the Dry Cimarron, which George still thought of as the Promised Land.

"When do I start?" he said.

CHAPTER 9

Buried Gold

"We'll bury it," Dr. Owen said to George.

On the ground in front of them lay three canvas bags full of gold—five thousand dollars' worth.

That was a lot of wealth in the 1880's, and there were outlaws in the neighborhood who wouldn't stop at anything to get their hands on it.

Dr. Owen himself had never seen so much gold at one time, and he had got it only through a piece of good luck. Some time before, he had bought a herd of cattle, and George had trailed it from Texas to the Dry Cimarron. There a man unexpectedly offered the three bags of gold for the entire herd.

Dr. Owen had planned to winter the cattle on his new ranch, then to sell them the following year. But the chance for a quick profit was too good to miss. Besides, he could get another herd up from Texas before snow fell—if he hurried. Why waste time taking the gold to the bank in Trinidad? Instead he decided to hide it and go off with his brother John in search of more cattle.

Dr. Thomas E. Owen.

Courtesy Aultman Studio, Trinidad, Colorado

John lashed one of the bags behind his saddle. The doctor took the second. George, with the third bag tied securely, swung up onto his horse. Across his lap he held a shovel. Then, trying to look as if they were out doing regular ranch work, they all rode off toward a high mesa. On the way they kept a sharp lookout for anyone who might be watching them. Word of the big sale could have reached members of the Coe gang or some other outlaws, and they would certainly wonder what Dr. Owen was going to do with the gold.

Near a ledge at the foot of the mesa one spot was especially well hidden by oak trees. There George dug a hole in the clay soil. Into it went the three bags. Over them he spread clay, then scattered leaves and twigs on top. Soon the place looked just the way it had before he started digging.

The three men noted landmarks and measured the distance from the gold to the ledge. Now there was nothing to do but worry. The Coe gang had their headquarters off to the east in No Man's Land. If these desperadoes appeared while Dr. Owen and his brother were away buying cattle, they might try to force George to tell them what had happened to the gold. The future he looked forward to did not include cooperating with bandits.

Once in a while, during the time the Owens were gone, George rode past the ledge at the base of the mesa. Everything under the oak trees was just as he had left it. When Dr. Owen returned at last with a new herd of cattle, he, too, visited the ledge. But he decided not to dig up the gold yet. He would leave it buried until the following spring, then use it to buy more cattle and to pay for work on the big house and barn that he planned to build.

All winter George had the secret hoard on his mind. When he went to town for supplies, he was careful never to let slip even a hint of it. Sometimes, if the ground was clear of snow, he rode out to check the place where the treasure lay.

Dr. Owen brought his wife Molly and their children to the ranch in late May, when the vegas were blue with irises. Very soon after that he asked George to go with him for the gold. At the right spot under the oaks George pushed his shovel into the ground.

Soon something besides clay was coming out of the hole—strands of thread that looked like canvas. More and more shreds appeared. But no gold.

"It's gone!" George gasped.

"Don't play jokes on me!" The doctor laughed. Then he looked into the hole and grew serious. Dropping to his knees, he began to scoop out clay with his bare hands. Still no bags appeared.

"Are you sure this is the right place?" the doctor demanded.

Pointing to the landmarks, George said nothing and thrust his shovel into the earth again. It made a scratching noise and turned up some grit instead of smooth clay.

Gravel, George thought. Still, he didn't remember finding any gravel when he dug here before. So he took a closer look.

His shovel was bringing up gold—tiny nuggets of gold!

On their knees now, George and Dr. Owen clawed out fistfuls of gold mixed with clay. Before long they had a pile of nuggets that seemed large enough to have filled the three bags they had buried.

But what had become of the bags themselves?

"I think I know!" George said, suddenly full of laughter.

He began to look into holes in the cliff. From the back of one tiny cave a pair of bright eyes peered at him. Putting on a glove, George reached in until he felt something soft.

His hand brought out strands of thread, thread that had once been part of the canvas in the bags.

Rodents had dug burrows into the disturbed clay, found the bags, and proceeded to chew them up and take them away. The threads made soft material for a nest. In the nest lay some of the shiny nuggets, too.

CHAPTER 10

Alone in the Promised Land

When George first came back to the Dry Cimarron, he found Candido Archuletta and Tony Cornay and all his other Mexican friends still there. But the Mingus family had moved away—nobody knew where—after Mrs. Mingus gave birth to twin boys who soon died of diphtheria.

Cattlemen who now lived in the Mingus house showed George a wooden marker at the babies' grave under some oak trees nearby. The marker had fallen over. George straightened it and wished there was more he could do for the people who had befriended him. Some of the newcomers to the valley were not at all like the Minguses. They disliked black people and showed their hostility. Once in a while a black man wandered by, but he never stayed long. George alone stayed, and he sometimes felt very much alone. He had some of the freedom he had set out to find when he left Texas, but he was paying a price for it.

However, he had a good job at Hereford Park, which was what everyone called Dr. Owen's ranch, because it was the first place in the area to raise Hereford cattle instead of longhorns. There George enjoyed learning to do things he had never done before. He drove a four-horse team and hauled big loads of lumber and bricks for the grand house that Dr. Owen was building on a little knoll beside the Dry Cimarron. The house had a wonderful view in every direction, and it stood high above any flood that might come down the river.

A bunkhouse for three cowboys was to stand nearby. George supervised the Mexican workmen as they made big adobe blocks and dried them in the sun, then laid them up in walls. Later he whitewashed one of the rooms for himself. On shelves along one wall he put his possessions—his Indian skull, his guitar and violin, a Bible that Mrs. Mingus had given him, and a growing collection of minerals and rocks. His rifle hung on the wall. So did some shiny things called hondas that he liked to carve from the horns of cattle.

To make a honda, George cut off a section of the hollow horn, then filed it and polished it. The smooth little cylinder was just the right size to hold together the ends of the bandanna George always wore around his neck. Hondas made good presents for his friends, too. So did spurs. George liked to buy them and give them as a reward to boys he trained when they became good bronc peelers or skillful ropers.

When he rode up to the big house, George often found Dr. Owen inspecting the progress that the builders were making on his home. The tall, stoop-shouldered physician was always going over plans, always ordering something new. One time he had a chair especially built with a frame made from the great curving horns of longhorn cattle. Another time George drove a buckboard all the way to Trinidad to get an organ the doctor had ordered. George enjoyed listening to Dr. Owen's wife Molly play songs on the instrument as she pumped air into it with her feet.

The Owen boys, Tom and Ben, were growing up. George began to teach them the tricks of riding and roping, just as he had taught the Roberds boys. Tom had a special knack for riding, and Ben was very good with the lariat. George gave them both the spurs he felt they had earned.

After the new house was finished, George ate with the Owen family in the big kitchen. At the Roberds ranch he had never sat down with white folks at meals, but the doctor was unusual in this as in other ways. Although he had been an officer in the Confederate Army, he had not owned slaves in Missouri, where he lived before he went West. George always felt that Dr. Owen really saw him when he looked at him, and what Dr. Owen saw was a man who had become the best all-around cowboy on the Dry Cimarron.

One evening the doctor sat in his longhorn chair with his saddlebags on his lap, checking the bottles of medicine he always carried. Some of them were not full; he had visited a man who had been badly injured when one of his feet caught in the stirrup as he was thrown from a half-wild horse. The doctor added chloroform to one bottle and opium to another, then checked his scissors and tweezers and surgical knives. As he tidied his kit, he talked with George about his plans.

"Ranchers are going to stop running cattle loose on the range," he said. "This year we'll have our last roundup. We've got to put a barbed-wire fence around the place. And you're in charge."

"I've never fenced with barbed wire," George said. "But I guess I can learn."

"I never saw the job you couldn't learn." The doctor tucked the bottles back in his saddlebags. "I've ordered the wire. It will get here after the railroad comes through."

For the final roundup, a dozen different ranches sent men to gather and brand their new calves. Each ranch had its own chuck wagon and ten or a dozen cowboys. And each cowboy had ten or a dozen horses in the remuda. One man, called a wagon boss, was in charge of the work for each ranch. George was wagon boss for Dr. Owen's two ranches. He had thousands of cattle to look after and more than two hundred horses.

It was also George's job to hire extra riders. A few of the cowboys who asked for work were black—the first he had met in many years. He was happy to see these men and quickly gave them jobs. His old dream that the valley of the Dry Cimarron could be the Promised Land for blacks who had been in bondage came back to life. Possibly some of these riders would like the country as well as he did. Maybe they would stay on.

To fill out the number of men he needed, George hired some white cowboys. They were all from Texas, and they looked as if they would rather shoot him than work for him. But they needed jobs, and the other roundup crews were full.

The Owen chuck wagon and remuda moved south past Capulin Mountain and then on farther south for several days to the place where all the wagons were to meet. Very soon George saw that the white cowboys he had hired were not settling down like the ones he had trailed north with years before. They were a mean bunch, continually trying to stir up trouble with the black riders. George had to make the best of an ugly situation. Since he had no time to teach the white cowboys how to act toward other human beings, he decided to keep blacks and whites apart as much as possible.

"You eat and sleep on this side of the wagon and leave the other side to them," he told the black cowboys the second night out. "If you don't, those Texans may arrange for a funeral, and one of you will be heading the procession in a pine box."

The first day of branding, George watched the men work. It was soon clear why the white cowboys had not been hired by the other wagon bosses. They didn't know their work. When they tried to rope calves, they almost always missed. They had no idea of how to handle a lariat.

Quietly George began to take part in the roping. His horse was well trained, and his loop never missed. The Texans, who resented having to work for a black boss, began to watch him with astonishment. Once, when an ornery cow wouldn't keep away from her calf, George took a second lariat and flicked it through the air, wrong-end-to. He'd made a whip of it, the way he had learned to do on trail drives long ago. The sting of the rope on her hide persuaded the cow to move away and let the branders do their work.

Somehow this quick and surprising trick settled matters. The Texans caused no trouble after that. They silently acknowledged that George McJunkin had the right to be boss.

When the roundup was over, George went to watch the Irish railroad workers laying track. One thing puzzled him: The roadbed had started far away in Texas, yet it ended up here just where it was supposed to end.

"How do they know where to put the tracks?" George asked Antine Meloche one day. Antine was a friend who owned the big TO Ranch.

"The same way I know where to put my fences," Antine answered. "They use a transit. Come by the ranch sometime and I'll show you."

The transit, George discovered, was a small telescope set on a tripod.

"How does it work?" he wanted to know.

Antine showed him how to focus the telescope and how to set it at different angles, sideways or up or down, and how to sight through it.

"It keeps my fences where they ought to be," Antine said. "So I have no arguments with my neighbors."

"I could use a thing like that at Hereford Park," George said. "I'm going to fence the whole place."

"Take it. It's yours," Antine said with a dramatic gesture.

George knew his friend well and was used to his big impulsive acts of generosity. Antine was rich and could do what he wanted. George took the transit and soon put it to work at Hereford Park. Sometimes Tom and Ben helped him when they weren't in school.

One fall day, while George was laying out the fence, a cold wind made him shiver. It also gave him an idea. He dropped work and rode to Candido Archuletta's place.

"Will you sell me two sheepskins?" he asked.

"Of course, my friend," Candido replied.

"I'm going to make a coat. The ones in the store aren't warm enough. And they're too short."

George chose two skins, heavy with fleece, and rode home. Putting the fleece side in, he shaped and stitched a coat, long enough to cover his legs and split up the back so he could wear it in the saddle. Then, to go over this inner coat, he made another from deerskin he had tanned himself. Nobody around had ever seen anything quite like it, but it was very warm.

After the fence was done, George often rode along the whole length of it to do any mending that might be necessary. Once in a while, wind blew a tree down and snapped the wire. Or cattle rustlers or horse thieves cut it. So George was in the saddle day after day, and as he rode, he often saw things that made him wonder. Odd-shaped rocks always interested him, and he liked to pick up specimens to add to the collection in his neat room. Time and again he wished he could find books that would explain why the rocks had so many different shapes and colors, why one kind was smooth and another rough.

Sometimes Dr. Owen could satisfy George's curiosity, but he was away from the ranch for long periods. None of the cowboys could tell George what he wanted to know.

The Mexicans, though, had answers to some of his questions about certain plants that interested him. They had lived in this country for a long time and knew ways to use plants for curing sickness. George listened to what they told him, and he also learned from Dr. Owen. When the doctor was not around, George sometimes took care of a cowboy who was sick or injured. He made special medicines for horses, too.

Up and down the valley more and more people got to know George and to like him, and George liked most of them. But something was lacking. No blacks had seen the promise in his Promised Land, not even one of the black cowboys who worked for him on the roundup. When the railroad came in, the men who built it were from faraway Ireland, although thousands of black men in nearby Texas needed jobs. Railroad companies would not hire blacks. George had not found any of his own people with whom to share the life he had grown to love. He was alone.

He wished he had a family, but how could he marry? There were no black women in the valley. George liked some of the young Mexican women, and they liked him, but Mexican men strongly opposed marriage of their womenfolk to non-Mexicans. On the other hand, if he and a white woman wanted to become husband and wife, the white men in the valley would not stand for that. They respected George as a skilled cowboy, but not one of them would like it if he married a white woman. They all had been taught—and still believed—that such a thing was wrong.

If George wanted a wife, he would have to move somewhere else to find her. That meant he might not be able to get the kind of work he liked. In fact, he might not find any work at all, because many black men were unemployed.

George remembered the joy he had felt when he was suddenly free—no longer a slave—free to work for wages. This freedom was precious, but it was not the only kind in the world. There was the freedom to marry, for instance, and that was beyond his reach. So he stayed on the Dry Cimarron, and remained

single. Maybe someday there would be enough freedom of all kinds, he thought, so that everybody
could have a fair share of it.

CHAPTER 11

Blizzard

One fall day in 1889, George threw his saddle aboard the train at Folsom, the town nearest Hereford Park. He got off at Clayton near the Pitchfork Ranch, which also belonged to Dr. Owen. George had made the fifty-mile trip between the two ranches many times on horseback. But that was before the railroad had come through. Now he thoroughly enjoyed whizzing across country he knew so well.

It was actually because of the railroad that he was going to Clayton today. Dr. Owen planned to send a lot of Pitchfork Ranch cattle to market by train, and George was going to help round them up on the open range. Only part of the land around Clayton had been fenced by the year 1889. Nor were there any fences to speak of east of the ranch in what is now called the Panhandle of Oklahoma. In those days it was called No Man's Land because it did not yet belong to any state or territory. It had no government, and anybody could run cattle there.

Twelve cowboys with more than a hundred horses and a cook and chuck wagon were waiting at the three-room adobe ranch house, and soon after George arrived this outfit headed into No Man's Land.

Dr. Owen's brother John was wagon boss. Day after day the men rode out from camp and made wide sweeps, bringing in all the cattle they found. Then, with the help of riders from the Cross Ells and the 101 ranches, they separated the animals according to brand.

The Pitchfork herd was made up mostly of four-year-old steers, ready to ship to market. Each day the herd grew until nearly twelve hundred steers had been rounded up. They were fat and healthy and worth a small fortune. Until their train was ready, John Owen ordered the men to hold the herd together where they could get plenty of good grass on Sweet Creek near Cottonwood Arroyo, not far from the little village of Mineral in No Man's Land.

On the morning of October 30, the weather turned chilly. George was glad he had remembered to bring along his sheepskin-buckskin winter coat. For good measure, he lashed his yellow slicker onto his saddle behind the cantle. All morning he rode slowly around the herd to make sure that none of the steers strayed away. That afternoon the rain he had feared began to fall. By evening the cowboys who didn't have slickers were soaked through, and everybody was cold.

Some of the men had dry clothes to change into,

but nobody stayed dry very long. The riders had to take turns circling around the herd in the dark, and during the night the rain turned to snow. Worst of all, the wind blew harder and harder.

Before George went out to help hold the herd together, he tore a strip off a blanket and wrapped it around his head to protect his face and ears. He wound other strips over his boots and gloves. His companions silently followed his example.

The more the wind blew, the more the cattle tried to move away from it, seeking some way out of the driving snow. When daylight came, the men and horses could see only a few feet in front of them, so thick were the flakes in the wind.

For two days and two nights the storm continued, while riders struggled to hold the herd—and to keep themselves from freezing. John Owen finally ordered the cook to harness the mules to the chuck wagon and move it along with the drifting cattle. The wrangler tried to keep the remuda together, but one by one the horses dropped out of sight.

George was thoroughly alarmed. He had never seen such a storm, and there was no sign of a letup. By the beginning of the third day, most of the horses were gone. The other cowboys were so numb with cold and exhaustion they could hardly ride. Snow still filled the air, and drifts had so changed the landscape that John Owen and all the white cowboys acknowledged that they were completely lost.

George had ridden over this country many times. In spite of the drifts, he thought he recognized landmarks and a fence that led toward the little adobe ranch house where a man named Harvy Bramblett lived. Bramblett's place was scarcely big enough to hold fourteen men, but it would be shelter, and it offered their only hope. If they didn't reach it, they would die of cold.

"We've got to give up the cattle." The wind was howling, and George had to shout to John Owen. "It's them or us."

John was too exhausted to answer.

"I think I can get us to Bramblett's," George called. "But everybody's got to stick together and follow me close."

"Try it," John said, surrendering his authority as boss of the crew.

George turned his weary horse and rode straight into the driving blizzard. The animal stumbled time and again as he broke a trail in snow that was two feet deep in some places and drifted higher than a man's head in others. George tried to encourage the horse with a word or two, but the wind blew the sound of his voice away.

Night came on, and with snow beating against his eyes, it was harder than ever to see, but George kept his direction by forcing the horse to go where it was hardest to go—into the wind.

He had begun to give up all hope of reaching shelter before night imprisoned them when a light flickered in the darkness ahead. It flickered again. This had to be the light that Harvy Bramblett—like any good rancher—put in his window whenever there was a storm.

"My God, how did you stay alive?" Harvy exclaimed when George stumbled through the door.

"We just about didn't," George replied, "and we wouldn't have, if you hadn't set your light where we could see it."

One after another the men sank to the floor, exhausted. They literally filled the one-room house, and Harvy could scarcely move around to make coffee.

He had just put in some of his winter supplies, so he was able to feed them all. They took turns sleeping on the floor, and every once in a while somebody would look out the window—until it was completely blocked with drifted snow.

The days wore on, and the fourteen men in the single room ate their way through Harvy Bramblett's winter food supply. By the tenth day of the blizzard, they were hungry. On the eleventh day the snow ended, and blinding sunlight poured down on a landscape that was completely without features.

The men got busy outside the rancher's house, shoveling paths to his barn and privy and sheds. Every one of the Pitchfork horses had frozen to death. So, apparently, had all the twelve hundred cattle. Weeks later, however, George and the other cowboys did find a few steers that had survived by drifting far to the south.

Dr. Owen had lost a fortune. Not only was the valuable Pitchfork herd gone, and all the horses with it, but many of the cattle at Hereford Park had died as well. George would have a great deal to do if he was to get Hereford Park running again. But as he faced the problem, he had the satisfaction of knowing that he had saved fourteen lives. And all of the men George had led to Bramblett's knew that they would have died if he had not taken charge.

CHAPTER 12

Manager

"George, hitch up the buggy and drive me to the train," Dr. Owen said.

Two years had passed since the blizzard, and both of them had worked hard to keep Hereford Park going. Now George was puzzled and alarmed. Did the doctor know what he was saying? He had just come from the train.

But the older man insisted, and George did as he was told. He could not appeal to Molly Owen, because she was at their Trinidad home with the four children.

When the doctor started to climb into the buggy, he slipped and fell against a wheel. George had to help him into the seat.

"Where are you going, Doctor?" George asked on the road leading to the railway station in Folsom.

"I'm going to Molly."

"I'll go with you," George said.

"No." This was an order.

"Then I'll get the stationmaster to telegraph ahead and tell Mrs. Owen to meet you."

The doctor didn't answer. He only slumped down in the buggy seat and was silent the rest of the way to town.

When George helped the old man onto the train, all he said was, "Thank you, George, thank you. I know you'll take good care of things."

George offered again to stay with him, but the doctor would not hear of it. He made sure that his saddlebags with their pouches full of medicines were beside him on the seat in the railroad car, and then the train took him away.

That was the last time George saw the man who had been his friend as well as his employer and teacher for many years. The doctor was dead when the train reached Trinidad.

With Dr. Owen gone, George had many new responsibilities. He took full charge of everything. Mrs. Owen was not well herself, and the boys, Tom and Ben, were not old enough to run the ranch. They still had many things to learn, and they needed their father. It became George's task to take his place, and George was glad to do so. He had always wanted sons of his own. Now he and the boys saw a great deal of each other.

George taught Ben and Tom about horses and cattle and about running a big ranch. As they worked, a chunky little white man often looked on. He was William H. Jack, an important person in the New Mexico cattle industry.

Jack liked the way George handled a rope and horses—and men. It happened that Jack needed someone to run the ranch he had bought adjoining Hereford Park, because he expected to be away from the place a good deal of the time. When he was satisfied that George was the best possible man for the job, he asked him to work as foreman.

George agreed. He would start as soon as Ben and Tom were able to manage Hereford Park by themselves.

When that day came, George moved a mile up the valley. There he found even greater responsibilities than he had had in the past—and greater opportunities. He felt he had taken still another step toward independence and freedom.

CHAPTER 13

Fair Play

Bill Jack started out branding his cattle with a big XYZ on their sides. Then he decided to use a new and simpler brand that looked like the track of a crow's foot. So his ranch became known as the Crowfoot.

The stock at the Crowfoot came by train from another ranch, the Oak Grove, which Bill Jack owned far away in the dry southern part of New Mexico near Silver City. Although George made only a brief visit to Oak Grove, certain things happened there that turned out to make a great difference in the rest of his life.

Work at the Oak Grove ranch in the semidesert was routine. Each day he was there George rode out from the big rambling adobe ranch house and looked for cattle among the scraggly shrubs that covered the surrounding hills. On Saturdays he knocked off and rode eleven miles to Silver City for a change of scene.

In some ways this frontier town reminded him of Dodge City. Many of the people hated blacks, but others treated him well. They were used to black men on horseback because a regiment of black cavalry had recently been stationed at nearby Fort Bayard, and the men often came to town.

On one trip to Silver City, George picked up a newspaper. Mrs. Jack noticed that he read it over and over again, so she gave him some magazines. After that the two of them often talked about things that interested them both—about rocks and the plants at Oak Grove, many of which were new to George, and why weather was the way it was. These discussions gave Mrs. Jack an idea. She wrote to her home in Illinois for a book about the stars and an encyclopedia that she owned. They would be waiting at the Crowfoot to surprise George when he returned.

When the time drew near for a train to take the cattle north, George decided to make a final visit to Silver City. As usual, he put on a fresh white shirt and a clean bandanna, pulled on his good pair of boots, and started out at an easy trot.

Before he had gone far, he saw four saddled horses off to one side of the road. There were no riders in sight, but a commotion seemed to be going on behind a clump of brush. Someone was yelling for help.

George spurred his horse toward the noise. Four Anglos, all strangers to him, were having a violent fight. Two of them held a third man, while the fourth pounded his face, then kicked him in the stomach.

Before any of them realized George was there, he had pulled his rifle from its scabbard and moved his nervous horse close to the struggling group. The three attackers were startled, but they held on to their victim, who was bleeding from the head and face.

"Pretty hot day for that kind of work, isn't it?" George said. As he spoke he shifted the rifle to a new position across his lap.

No answer.

"Why three against one?" George asked.

"Go away, nigger, and tend to your own business," one of the men growled.

None of them carried guns, but there were rifles on all the saddles. When one of the trio looked as if he was going to jump toward the horses, George tapped his own rifle.

"You just stand where you are," he said calmly. Then he added, "I don't happen to like to see people killing each other."

George took a moment to glance at the injured man, who was obviously groggy and in pain, and that split second was all one of the bullies needed. He gave a terrific kick at the underbelly of George's horse. The frightened animal jumped aside and bucked at the same time. George, taken by surprise, lost his seat and landed in the dust.

Before he could regain his feet or find his rifle, which had gone flying, the three men had mounted their horses and sent the fourth horse running wildly away. A cloud of dust rose behind them as they galloped off in the direction of Lordsburg.

"You all right?" George asked the battered man.

"I think so," he replied without much conviction. "You came just in time. They would have killed me if you hadn't shown up."

"Why didn't they use their guns? That would have been easier."

"They wanted me to talk." The man paused. "They stopped me because they thought I was carrying an Army payroll. When they found I wasn't, they tried to make me tell who is carrying it. I couldn't have told them if I'd wanted to. I don't know. All I know is the money should be coming by train. Somebody must have told them a yarn and they believed it."

"Your head is still bleeding," George interrupted. "You'd better get to town right away."

The man seemed uncertain, but George caught his horse and helped him into the saddle, which had no horn in front. It was the kind of saddle the cavalry used. At that moment, George realized that the man was in uniform. Before, he had noticed only the dust and blood. Now he saw the insignia of a lieutenant.

"I'll stay with you till we get to Silver City. You don't look too good to me. Besides, those fellows might circle around and surprise you if I rode on ahead to get help," George said. "If they see both of us with rifles ready, they may be careful."

"I don't have a rifle," the officer said, and George

was perplexed. The man was now on his right, but George was sure he had seen a rifle scabbard fastened to the far side of his saddle.

The officer was in too much pain to ride at a trot, and so the horses had to walk. Gradually he became more alert. When they reached a place where the road topped a rise, he stopped and looked back. From this point a great sweep of land lay open to the south. After a quick glance over the whole scene, the lieutenant reached into his scabbard and took out, not a rifle, but a telescope. It was almost two feet long, and when extended, it was still longer.

Putting the telescope to his eye, he searched the road where it showed on a bare low ridge in the distance. At length he seemed to find what he was looking for.

"Those fellows are still headed for Lordsburg," he said. "They'll probably swing wide of the town and keep on going south to the border. They'll be in Mexico before anyone can catch them."

"They weren't Mexicans," George said.

"I know. Just one-hundred-percent-American highway robbers," the lieutenant said as he collapsed his telescope.

George had never seen such an instrument before. It was much larger than the little one on his surveyor's transit.

"Could I look at that thing?" he asked.

The man handed it to George, then showed him how to adjust it.

The view through the lenses was astonishing. Distant trees became large and close, and George, too, saw the three horsemen, still heading south.

George turned a bit in the saddle. Off to the west were some cattle he could just see with his naked eye. Through the telescope he could actually read their brands.

"XYZ!" he exclaimed. "Bill Jack's old brand. Those are strays from the Oak Grove Ranch where I work."

The telescope was a marvelous instrument. It moved him up close to everything in the distance, made him feel able to escape from some of the ordinary limitations of life. This curious sense of freedom—of power—was exciting and very different from the explosive feelings that had burst out of him when freedom from slavery came on that June day many years ago.

"You like it?" the lieutenant asked. "It's yours. You can have it. You deserve a lot more than that."

George hesitated.

"I mean it. The telescope is yours." The young man was obviously in earnest.

"Thank you," George said, feeling uncomfortable. He slipped the telescope into his rifle scabbard and kept his rifle on his lap.

In town he rode with the injured man to the café, where soldiers from Fort Bayard gathered on Saturday. The men clustered around the officer.

"Apaches on the warpath?" one asked. It wasn't a silly question. Troops at Fort Bayard had fought Apaches not very long before that.

Another soldier seemed to be good at first aid. He took care of the injured man and commandeered a buggy in which to drive him to the surgeon at the fort.

Some of the men had enough whiskey in them to think that the best thing was to ride off in pursuit of the highway robbers. With a corporal taking command, they lined up on their horses in double file, and George was sure they were more concerned with keeping in formation than with anything else. They would be back soon, none the worse for their ride—and without any captured robbers.

That day George didn't look up his friends in town. He went straight to a saddle shop and waited while the Mexican saddlemaker put a scabbard on the left side of his saddle. Now he had two. Into one he slid his rifle and into the other went the telescope.

From now on he would be able to spot cattle farther away than any other cowboy in New Mexico. And he soon found also that he could see things in the night sky that he had not dreamed were there when he told time by the stars on the trail drive during his turns at night herding.

The world around George McJunkin had grown larger now that he had a long brass tube called a telescope.

CHAPTER 14

Foreman on the Crowfoot

As he and Candido and other cowboys drove the XYZ cattle from Folsom to the Crowfoot Ranch, George thought the countryside had never looked better. It was spring, and it was good to be home, and he burst out singing. The tune he sang was one he had heard on roundups in No Man's Land years before:

Range is getting grassy, winter's drawed its claws,
Calves are fat and sassy, teasing of their ma's,
Laughing days are over, dreaming days are gone,
No more life in clover, for the roundup's on.

Come along, you fellows, hear the foreman shout,
Drop your books and banjos, fetch your saddles
  out,
Put away them card decks, wrangle up your traps,
Get your spurs and ropes, buckle on your chaps.

George McJunkin about 1911.

No more northern blizzards, weather's soft and
  prime,
Nature's fairly yelping that it's roundup time.

After the last of the XYZ herd passed the gate of
the Crowfoot, George discovered he was doing more
and enjoying more than ever before. Daytimes he
had full charge of an eight-thousand-acre ranch. At
night he fixed up his room in the adobe house he
shared with Mr. and Mrs. Jack when they were there.

A big fireplace almost filled one side of George's
room. On the mantel he set the Indian skull he had
been carrying around for years. Above that, he hung
the head of a deer he had stuffed. On the mantel
with the skull lay his collection of crystals and
stones and minerals and a few Indian arrowheads.

Beside the fireplace he built shelves, one for his
fiddle and guitar, others for books, including his
Bible and the encyclopedia and the book on stars
that Mrs. Jack had given him. Finally he gave the
room a fresh coat of whitewash, spread a bearskin on
the floor, and began to feel very much at home.

But his tinkering went on. One time, using information he found in the encyclopedia, he built a
gauge to measure rain. Another time he rigged up a
small windmill so that he could measure how fast
the wind was blowing. Later he made room on the
shelf for a carving he found in a shed on the ranch.
The artist who made it had once been a partner of
Bill Jack, and apparently he had forgotten to take it
when he moved out.

The figures in the carving showed seven different

stages in the life of a man. First there was a baby, then a boy, then a teen-ager. After that came a young man in a soldier's uniform, a middle-aged man who looked like a businessman, a thin old man, and finally a very old man in his second childhood. George often thought about the figure of the middle-aged man. He himself was well past fifty now, older than the fellow in the carving, but there was a difference. The carved figure had a big stomach; George was as slender as he had always been. He didn't weigh a pound over 160.

The house George lived in had been the home of young Mr. and Mrs. Mingus, who had befriended him so long ago. It reminded him of much in the past. The Bible Mrs. Mingus had given him was now so battered that he had to tie a string around it to keep the pages together. In the oak grove near the house, the headboard over the Mingus babies' grave had fallen down again. Obviously it would keep falling down, so George decided to replace it with a stone marker. He ordered one made, and when it was ready he hauled it from Folsom in the ranch wagon and set it in place. Then he planted a rosebush and built a fence around the grave to keep the cattle out.

Next to the house George put up a log building to serve as a blacksmith shop. Here he shod the horses and repaired the ranch wagon and sharpened picks and axes. The glow in the forge and the horsey smell made him think of his father's shop. But it did not make him want to go back to Texas. Here, as master of many skills and foreman of a large ranch, he enjoyed much greater freedom than would have been possible if he had stayed where night riders kept blacks from getting schools.

On Johnson Mesa, where the timber grew tall and big, George cut trees and sawed them into beams for a barn. He also found a spring that flowed all year round. With his transit he traced a route for bringing water down to the ranch house, more than a mile away. Then he laid pipe that whole distance. There was more water than he needed in the house, so he built a dam nearby to form a pond where the stock could drink even when the river dried up.

People who came to the ranch always found George busy, always in a clean white shirt. Most cowboys wore gray shirts for work, but George liked white ones. Quite simply, they said to the world, "Here is a man so skillful that he can handle a difficult job without getting all messed up." He even wore a white shirt when he branded cattle or gelded male horses. This job of castrating horses was done in order to make them easier to handle. George had learned from Dr. Owen how to perform the operation. The doctor had shown him how to avoid cutting the large blood vessels and how to prevent infection. George was so good at gelding that ranchers in the whole area asked him to do the work for them.

More than once George found a calf that had been killed by a wolf, and that always called for a wolf hunt. He also hunted bear and deer and antelope. Once when he was with Candido Archuletta he shot six deer. The next day, many Mexican families in the valley had venison to eat. George felt very close to the Mexicans. They and he both were nonwhite, and because of that they had many experiences in common.

As he hunted or rode out looking for stray cattle, George often found land that no one owned. In one place a good spring flowed from the mountainside. Good grazing land surrounded it. A man could live here and water some stock and build up a ranch of his own. Old dreams of independence turned into a new dream of becoming a self-employed rancher. Now it seemed possible to bring this dream to life. In those days any citizen could get a homestead—160 acres of government land—free if he built a cabin on it and showed that he was using the place. George built his cabin and in time got his land. At last he hoped to run his own cattle and take orders from no man.

But there was a catch. Cowboys did not earn much money, and George had always been generous with what he had. Now, when he needed cash to buy cattle, he had none. Hope of being his own boss had to be postponed.

No one knows exactly what happened, but it seems likely that Bill Jack offered to sell cattle to George and to let him run them on the Crowfoot, if George would add his land to the Crowfoot. Whatever the details were, Jack did become owner of the homestead. George put his own brand—three quarter-circles 〰 —on a few cows. Each year he branded the calves borne by his cows, and steadily his herd grew.

George had plans for his herd. He was going to sell it, when it was large enough, and use the money to build a house in Folsom.

"I'll live there when I marry or get old," he said.

By now he had a good many friends in town. Often when he went there for supplies he put a quarter of newly slaughtered steer in the wagon. The meat sometimes went to Mrs. Martinez who washed his shirts. Or he might give it to the family of some Mexican man who had been killed. Every once in a while an Anglo would get drunk and shoot a Mexican. One sheriff in Folsom said he knew of a hundred such killings, but he didn't know of a single Anglo who had been found guilty of murder.

George had Anglo friends, and he helped them, too. If a cowboy couldn't buy a railroad ticket when he had to go off looking for work, George gave him money. And every boy and girl in Folsom bought candy at some time or other with nickels George had given them. So much generosity made it hard to save money for his house. Still he managed to put a little aside, and he kept on planning.

On the Fourth of July, George always went to town. Everybody did. There was something to do all day long. Boys and girls ran foot races. Men pulled gunnysacks over their feet and legs and had a sack race, hopping as fast as they could. Little red firecrackers popped and sputtered. Sometimes a big one made a great bang when a boy set it off inside a tin can. The smell of exploding powder mixed with the smell of food and dusty streets.

In the afternoon cowboys had a potato race. Holding long, pointed sticks, they lined up their prancing horses along one end of a field. At the crack of a starting gun they dashed to the other end of the field, where a lot of potatoes had been scattered on the ground. Each rider tried to spear one and gallop back with it to the starting line. It was hard to spear a potato, and even harder to keep it on a stick, because everybody tried to knock everybody else's off.

George, in his white shirt, raced with the others. He didn't always win, but he had a good time.

At the regular horse races that followed the potato race George usually had a special job to do. He held the bets. That meant he stood beside the field and listened to other men's guesses about the winner. If one said to another, "I'll give you three dollars for two that Jose Gonzalez wins," George would take three dollars from one man and two from the other. After the race he would hand all the money to the man who had guessed right. Old-timers in Folsom knew that George would pay the winner what the winner should get.

Newcomers in town, however, often brought prejudices with them. Sometimes they said stupid, insulting things about black men. George paid no attention. At least he didn't seem to pay attention. But he had his own way of laughing at people who laughed at him.

One such stranger found George sitting in the

lobby of the hotel in Folsom. Slyly George took a newspaper, held it upside down, and pretended to be studying it.

"I see that all my kinfolks are going to die," George announced, as if he were commenting on a news story.

"What are you talking about?" the stranger demanded. He had the special look on his face that meant, "This dumb nigger obviously can't read."

"All blacks got blackleg," George answered solemnly, saving his laughter till later. George's friends all knew that blackleg was a disease that killed cattle, and sure enough, they told him, the stranger reported that George had pretended to read news about an epidemic while he held the paper upside down.

Another time two men from the East, who had just bought a ranch near Capulin Mountain, came into a café where George was sitting with some of his friends.

"Get that nigger out of here," one of the Easterners ordered the proprietor.

"Nothing doing! If you don't like it here, you can leave."

"I never yet sat down with a nigger," the Easterner said angrily, "and I'm not going to start now."

"We'll find you a seat where George won't bother you," one cowboy said. He rose from the table, and others followed him. A moment later both strangers were sitting in a puddle in the middle of the street.

George stood at the café window, watching. Then something happened that sent chills through him.

One of the cowboys had grabbed a whip from a wagon that stood nearby. The sight of one man about to lash another brought to George's mind a scene from his childhood. Once when his owner sent him on an errand to a neighbor's place he had seen the master there whipping a slave. The spectacle had filled him with horror, and when, for some reason, the slave owner turned on George and threatened to have him beaten, too, George had fled.

Now he ran out of the café into the street. "Whoa! Save your whip for those dumb mules you drive," George said.

"What they said ain't right," one cowboy protested.

"It ain't right to drink warm beer," George replied. "And yours is getting warm. Come on in now."

The two newcomers disappeared down the street. They had made a bad start in the community. Later they wanted to wipe out the memory of this affair, so they invited everybody to a dance at their ranch. Word went around that there would be plenty of food and drink.

The ranchers tried to get musicians. Several men in town played the fiddle but every one of them refused to play at the party.

The ranchers began to worry. "Don't you know anyone who can fiddle?" one of them asked Candido Archuletta.

"Sure, I know the best fiddler in the country," Candido answered.

"Well, bring him along, then."

Candido laughed, and George surprised everyone by coming to the party and playing all night. Later he explained.

"A fiddle is a better teacher than a whip," he said. "Besides, I only charged double my usual price for playing."

CHAPTER 15

The Telescope

For many years after George McJunkin got his telescope, he carried it in the scabbard attached to the left side of his saddle. When he was looking after cattle on the huge Crowfoot Ranch, he often stopped on a high point and peered through the spyglass. He could clearly see animals that were two, three, even four miles away. From the top of one particular mesa on the Stuyvesant Springs Ranch, where Crowfoot cattle and horses often grazed, George could keep a good eye on much of the stock under his care.

At night he found another use for the instrument. He would stretch out on the ground, with his head on his saddle, and search the skies through the telescope. At first he just enjoyed seeing how big and bright were the stars that he had come to know when he kept time by them on a trail drive. Then he began to wonder about other stars he was seeing for the first time. There were maps of the sky in the star book Mrs. Jack had given him. Using these, he learned to name a great many of the little points of light that dotted the heavens on clear summer nights.

Cowboys were so used to seeing George with his telescope at any hour of the day or night that they would have found nothing strange about his presence on Johnson Mesa one fall afternoon, or about his interest in the patches of scrub oak below. Cattle sometimes wandered in among the trees, and it was not always easy to find them there. If grass was scarce, as it was right then, the cattle had to be kept out of the groves. A hungry steer or cow might nibble the oak leaves, and the leaves could make it sick. Indeed it might die.

But George wasn't looking for cattle on this particular day. He sought a man, armed and dangerous. No one knew who this person was, but he had killed the wife of José Griego, a sheep rancher farther west. Apparently the murderer had gone to the sheep ranch looking for money. At that time of year, José Griego paid off his herders, and he had quite a lot of cash on hand.

Yet José found all his money just where he had hidden it. His wife had kept his secret—but lost her life. And the murderer had fled.

George now stood lookout with his telescope in case the man came to the Crowfoot Ranch, where Mrs. Jack was staying, or to Hereford Park, where Mrs. Owen might be alone with her daughter Edna. Tom and Ben, her sons, could very well be away.

All afternoon George kept his telescope trained on the country through which the man would be likely to go in order to reach the Crowfoot or the Owen ranch. Then, when the shadows grew long, he saw cattle moving nervously near one cluster of trees. A bluejay flew up suddenly from the same grove.

To George these signs meant that something was going on. It might be a bear that had wandered down off the mesa looking for berries or honey. It might be a bobcat or a wolf—or a man. If it was a man, then he had come on foot. A rider would have been visible among the low oak trees.

Quietly George shifted his horse along the side of the mesa so that he could get a different view of the country below. A sudden glimpse of movement stopped him. Through the telescope he saw a man—a stranger with a rifle in one hand and a lariat in the other. The stranger edged toward a horse that was grazing on the range, ready to rope it. Could this be the murderer? Perhaps he had started out on foot and now he wanted to steal a horse for a faster getaway after dark.

George slid his telescope into the scabbard on the left side of his saddle. Then he dismounted, pulled his rifle from the scabbard on the right, and began to move quietly down the slope.

At almost the same moment the stranger roped the horse and led it through the brush. After tying it to a tree, he set off toward the house on the Crowfoot Ranch.

"He wants a bridle and saddle," George thought.

There was no time to waste. He ran back, mounted quickly, and circled around to the ranch house out of the man's sight. To George's surprise and relief he found that Mrs. Jack had driven to town in the buggy. A note on the mantel said she would stay overnight with friends.

George grabbed all the bridles in the barn and hid them under the hay. There were only two saddles in sight. He hid both. In the house, Bill Jack's rifle and revolver hung over the mantel. Usually George did not bother with a revolver, but today was different. He strapped it on; then, with one rifle in the scabbard and the other across his lap, he set out for the Owen ranch house.

He didn't follow the road. That would take him too close to the place where he had last seen the suspicious stranger. At one place the fence stood in his way. He used his clippers to cut the wire and, not pausing to repair the break, rode on at a gallop. As he approached the big white house high on its knoll, he slowed his mount to a walk. At the barn he led the horse into a stall where it would be out of sight. Then he walked quietly to the house and leaned his rifles against the wall by the kitchen door.

"Mrs. Owen," he called. "You got a cup of coffee for a thirsty cowboy?"

"Why, George! You surprised me!" Mrs. Owen answered. "Of course I've got coffee. There's fresh pie, too."

George sat down at the big kitchen table.

"Where are the boys?" he asked.

"They went to the Pitchfork to help with the haying this week."

"Did Edna go, too?"

"No, she's outside someplace, rounding up cattle."

George knew what that meant. Edna would be astride a stick, galloping around in the dust pretending she was a cowboy.

"Mrs. Owen, you tell Edna to come in right now. Then I want you to stay in the house, too." George was speaking quietly and in a tone of voice Mrs. Owen had never heard before.

"Is something the matter? You're acting very strange."

"There's a bad man loose, and he may be headed this way. I'm going to stay right here so you'll be all right."

Mrs. Owen called Edna and took her upstairs. After closing the barn door, George got his two rifles and went into the house. Part of the time he stood in the kitchen, looking out the window. Part of the time he stood on the large screened-in porch. In between, he moved around, making noises. If a stranger came near the house, he would probably think there were several men there.

Edna didn't know what was going on, but she liked having her supper upstairs for a change, and she enjoyed being read to until she fell asleep.

All night long, George kept stirring around, peering out into the dark. Once he thought he saw a figure beside the stone tower that held up the water tank. But no one approached the house, and when daylight came, there was no one in sight.

George walked out to the water tower. Had he

been imagining things? He had not! There on the ground were the prints of boots, and the prints were fresh. George followed them toward the river. Near the stream bank the man had mounted a horse, crossed over, and headed up toward the mesa.

Back in the barn George found his own horse still in its stall, Nothing around the whole place had been disturbed. The intruder had apparently decided not to risk a fight with all those men he had heard rattling around in the house!

George told Mrs. Owen that she was safe—that the man had gone on by.

"I'm going to follow him," he added.

"Please—don't take any risks!"

"Careful is my middle name," George replied, smiling. "Don't worry."

All morning he followed the tracks up the mesa. About noon he came to a small cabin where a bear hunter named Youngblood lived. There seemed to be an unusual amount of excitement stirring for such an isolated spot. A number of saddled horses stood with their reins dangling. On the far side of the cabin, men had gathered around a piece of canvas that covered something on the ground.

One of the men, George knew, was the sheriff. The others wore the badges of deputies.

"What's up?" George asked.

"We just got the man who murdered José Griego's wife," one of the deputies replied.

"How do you know he's the one?" George asked.

"We've sent for José to identify him," the deputy

said. He lifted a corner of the canvas. George could see that the dead man was a Mexican—the same man he had watched through the telescope the day before.

Then a sickening doubt came to George. How could he or the deputy—or anyone—be sure that this dead man was the murderer? José Griego had been away from home when his wife was killed. Neither José nor anyone else had been a witness to the crime.

But that wasn't all. Now George remembered something he had not thought about yesterday when he was on the lookout. Recently he had heard that a number of Mexicans who had always lived on land off to the west had been driven away from their homes by armed agents of a new landowner. George hoped that the dead man—the man he, as well as the sheriff's posse, had suspected—was not simply a poor Mexican fleeing from a rich Anglo.

George looked up at the deputies. For a moment he saw not their hard faces but the masks of night riders out of his childhood back in Texas.

CHAPTER 16

Flood

After the Crowfoot Ranch got a telephone, George liked to joke with the operator. In those days phones were not automatic. Each one had its own little crank, which had to be turned by hand. When George twirled the crank on his instrument, a bell jangled in the home of Mrs. Sarah Rooke, the telephone operator in Folsom, eight miles away.

"Number, please?" came Mrs. Rooke's voice.

"Give me that hole in the wall," George would say with a chuckle.

Mrs. Rooke would then connect him with the little café that was run by redheaded Elbert Davis, a good friend of George.

When Elbert called George, he never gave the number of the Crowfoot Ranch. He just told Mrs. Rooke, "Get me Blackleg Ranch," and she knew what number to ring.

Mrs. Rooke was an important person in town. Every phone call in the area went through her switchboard. She told people the time when they called to ask. She took messages for those who weren't at home. She passed along news of all kinds.

On the afternoon of August 27, 1908, George had some urgent news he wanted to pass on. He had been up on Johnson Mesa that day when clouds began to gather; the sky had then turned very dark. That was a bad sign. It looked like a cloudburst coming.

On the way back to the ranch house, he had decided he ought to phone Sarah Rooke and tell her about the storm. It might be bright and sunny eight miles away in Folsom, and people there would never suspect that a cloudburst on the mesa could make the river rise during the night.

Rain had started to fall by the time George put his horse in the barn. It was still afternoon, but the clouds were so black that he had to light his kerosine lamp. This done, he cranked the little handle on his phone.

However, Mrs. Rooke did not answer with her cheery "Number, please?"

George cranked again. Still no answer. Another try and he gave up. The line must be out of order. It often was.

Real darkness came, and the storm continued. The patter of raindrops turned to heavy thuds as water in great clots fell on the roof. Never in his life had George heard such a downpour, and he began to worry about cattle that might be near the river. The rising water could trap some of them. But it would be impossible to find animals in the total darkness of this blinding storm.

Restless and worried, George put on a slicker and went out. His lantern cast only a dim glow, but he could see that the earth dam was still holding the pond near the house. However, water flowing over the top was beginning to dig little gullies. If the gullies grew deeper, the dam might wash away. Then he would have the whole hard job of building it up again.

Grabbing some gunnysacks and a shovel from the barn, George ran to the pond. Perhaps he could fill the sacks with mud and use them to stop the erosion. But water came flooding into the little reservoir faster and faster. As soon as he filled a gully in one place, a new channel formed somewhere else. He couldn't save the dam.

Neither could he save any of the stock that were sure to be in trouble by now. All he could think of doing when he got back to the house was to put a pan on the floor under a leak that had begun in the roof.

Later he went out to check his rain gauge. It was overflowing—and the dam was gone. George struggled on toward the barn. Rushing water, halfway up to his boot tops, poured from higher ground. Under it, the earth had turned to deep, slippery mud. A flowing muddy sheet covered the barn floor. But the horse was still safe. That was something.

George struggled out well beyond the barn, which sat on the edge of a slope. He was sure he heard tumbling noises, different from thunder—and there was plenty of that. A flash of lightning gave him a glimpse of a heavy tree thumping end over end like a tumbleweed. By now the river itself must be rising above its banks. A great flood was sweeping down the valley. And there was nothing he could do.

By morning the rain had stopped, but the roar of water had not. George saddled his horse and soon after daybreak set out down the valley. Where he could have jumped across the little river yesterday it now spread out a hundred yards wide. In some places it was even wider than that, and it looked like boiling liquid mud, full of the soil that had washed down off the mesa.

The big white ranch house at Hereford Park was safe on its knoll. But there was no hope for any cattle or horses that might have been out on the wide vegas near the stream. George stopped only long enough to make sure the Owens were all right, then rode on.

The railroad bridge at Folsom was gone. In a house on high ground George found a woman who could tell what had happened. For a while, she said, the bridge with its embankments at both ends had acted as a dam holding back the water. But about midnight this dam gave way. When daylight came, the town was hardly recognizable. Half the buildings had disappeared. Water ran two, three, four feet deep in the streets, and no one knew where many of the townspeople were.

"Men have gone out to look," the woman said. She was red-eyed from weeping.

George turned to leave.

"Can I come with you?" a boy called out. George recognized him. He was Dee Shoemaker, who lived north of the Crowfoot on Johnson Mesa.

"How come you're here?" George asked.

"Dad brought me down. He's out rescuing."

George hesitated. If Dee's father had not taken him on the search, maybe George had better not.

"I'll come back later and we'll talk about it," George said and rode away.

Later he was glad he hadn't taken the boy. He and other men doing rescue work soon found the bodies of people who had drowned. The number of dead kept mounting—ten, twelve, fifteen.

"Nobody has seen Sarah Rooke," one of the men reported when it grew too dark to continue the search. "She kept phoning and warning everybody until the lines went down." Even her house had vanished—washed away.

It didn't matter that George's call had not gone through. Sarah Rooke had heard about the flood from someone else—and now she was beyond rescue. So was Lucy, the sister of Ben Owen's wife.

The flood had destroyed much of the little town of Folsom, and it devastated many ranches along the river. Now, like everyone else in the valley, George had an immense job to do—rebuilding.

CHAPTER 17

Discovery

George had been alone on the Crowfoot Ranch at the time of the flood. Charley Wiley, who helped him break horses, had been away. But then Charley came and went as he pleased. Sometimes George felt that this young fellow needed to be taught a few things, just as much as the wild horses did.

"Charley's scarcely even rough-broke," George said, but he was patient. Besides, he did need help. He was fifty-seven years old, no longer young enough to ride the toughest broncs.

Right now, Charley, with George's guidance, was gentling a beautiful horse named Kalicrates. The two of them rode along a gully that George called Wild Horse Arroyo, because he often took broncs to that part of the ranch when he was training them. The arroyo had been only two or three feet deep before the flood. Now it was ten feet deep—in some spots even deeper. A fence that had crossed it before the flood now dangled high over empty space. George

A photograph of the Folsom Site in 1927, taken by Frank H. H. Roberts, Jr.

studied the fence and wondered how he could fix it so that the stock would not be able to go under it in the bottom of the arroyo.

In the gully wall, the roots of plants had been washed bare by flood water. Below them, a white object caught George's eye.

"I'm going to have a look down there," he said to Charley.

What had caught his attention turned out to be a large bone that stuck out of the side of the arroyo about ten feet below the surface of the ground. Around the large bone were smaller ones.

"Toss me the barb-wire clippers," George called to Charley.

With the clippers he scraped earth from around the big bone.

"Looks like a buffalo," he announced to Charley, who was much more interested in live broncs than he was in dead bones. "But it's the biggest buffalo bone I ever saw—and I've seen plenty of them in my day."

George wrapped the bone in his slicker and tied the bundle onto his saddle behind the cantle. That night he set it beside the skull on the shelf above his fireplace.

Every time he looked in the arroyo, he saw ribs or skulls or vertebrae jutting from the wall, and he began to call the place the Bone Pit. What had happened there? Why were there so many bones? And why were the bones so oversized? Nobody around Folsom knew the answer.

The more George saw of these strange things, the more curious he became. One day he heard that there was a man in Las Vegas who knew a great deal about old bones, so George wrote him a letter about his discovery. But the man never came to have a look.

The cowboys he talked to in Folsom weren't much interested in the mystery, and they teased George a little about it. But George paid no attention. He collected more specimens and put them on his mantel. Everyone who visited him examined the bones, but no one had an explanation, not even Mrs. Jack.

One evening as he sat in front of the fireplace, George read a chapter in Deuteronomy, his favorite book in the Bible. He was enjoying the part that talked about a land of giants. "Giants dwelt therein in old time," it said. "And the Ammonites call them Zam-zum-mims."

George smiled. Zam-zum-mims—a good name for the giant bones he had found. The idea amused him, but it didn't answer any questions about his discovery. How did those skeletons come to be so deep in the ground? Mrs. Jack couldn't answer that, either, nor could a young nephew of hers who came from Illinois to visit the Crowfoot. He knew nothing about them, even though he was going to college and studying science.

As for George, long after he had dug out that first big bone he continued to be curious about his discovery.

CHAPTER 18

Horseless Carriages and Flying Machines

Up to the year 1912, no automobile had ever traveled along the rough dirt road from Folsom to the Crowfoot. However, George had seen and marveled at two or three of these horseless carriages when he visited the town of Raton. And now he was going back there to see something even more wonderful. A flying machine was going to put on a show at the fair!

Merchants in Raton were also offering a prize for the best old-time chuck wagon exhibited at the fair. Ever since the big roundup on the open range had ended, cowboys no longer needed to camp for a month or two at a time far from ranch headquarters, and chuck wagons were already something of a curiosity. George still had one. He had kept it in a shed under a roof, so it wasn't badly weathered.

Before the fair, he pulled the old wagon out and fixed it up. He polished the rust from its iron bolts and from its straps and braces. He greased the axles,

Carl Schwachheim at the Schwachheim home and blacksmith shop in Raton, New Mexico. In the background is
the elk horn fountain.

Courtesy Mrs. Tillie Schwachheim Burch

scraped off flakes of old paint, and brushed on new.
He put ancient iron kettles in the pot rack on top of
the chuck box at the rear of the wagon. Under the
chuck box he hung those cast-iron pots called Dutch
ovens. He filled compartments and drawers with
plates, knives, forks, spoons, cups. In one com-

partment he stored a record book, along with a brand book that showed his own brand—three quarter-circles.

Into the front part of the wagon he threw his bedroll, and then he said to young Dee Shoemaker, "How would you like to toss in your bedroll and go to the fair?"

Dee took off at a gallop toward his home on the mesa, and very soon he reappeared with his bedroll.

George drove four roan horses hitched to the chuck wagon, and Dee rode most of the way on the seat beside him. Dee's own horse, Bluebonnet, followed behind the wagon, tied alongside Headlight, George's saddle horse.

The forty-mile trip was hard on one wheel. Its iron tire came loose. In Raton, George had to hunt up a blacksmith who could fix it. He could have done the job himself back at the ranch, but here he did not have the right tools.

"I'll let you out by the railroad station," he said to Dee. "Meet me tonight at the fairgrounds. We'll put our bedrolls down there."

Dee hopped off the wagon, eager to see the sights.

At the edge of town George located a blacksmith shop run by a man named Schwachheim and his son Carl. Carl went to work on the wheel. And that was the beginning of a series of events that would put the names of George McJunkin and Carl Schwachheim into many an important scientific book.

As George waited at the door of the shop, he studied a fountain in the yard. Its top was decorated with two huge sets of elk antlers, interlocked, each imprisoning the other.

"Those are mighty fine antlers," George said. "Where'd you get them?"

"Up on Johnson Mesa," Carl replied. "Looks like two bull elk were in a fight. Their horns got locked together so they couldn't pull apart, and they both died. Did you ever see such big ones?"

"Never saw bigger," George admitted. "But I've seen the bones of animals that were plenty big enough to hold them up." He was thinking of the Bone Pit, and he went on to tell Carl about the giant buffalo remains.

Carl was a collector, too. No matter where he went, he picked up all kinds of bones and fossils and arrowheads. He kept a diary full of observations about birds, animals, flowers—every wild thing that inhabited the New Mexico mountains and plains.

"Where do you find those bones of yours?" Carl asked.

George described the location of the Bone Pit in Wild Horse Arroyo.

"If I ever get time off from work—and if somebody gives me a ride—I'll come out there," Carl said. He had no horse, and no automobile, either. There were only three cars in all of Raton.

"I'll be glad to show you the place," George said. At last he had found someone who was interested in his discovery. He paid for the repair work and drove off toward the fairgrounds to find Dee.

Next morning he lined up his wagon with a dozen

others and opened out the chuck box ready for inspection.

"You win," the judges told him. They gave him a new hunting rifle as a prize, and he had the honor of leading the parade that day.

Dee rode Bluebonnet and George sat on the wagon seat. Both of them liked being at the head of the parade, hearing people all along the street clap as they went past. Dee did most of the waving when there were cheers, but George waved, too.

Just as exciting as the parade was the sight of the flying machine. Not only did it fly, it did stunts as well. It rolled over and flew upside down. Then one of the flyers climbed out and stood on a wing. Finally it turned a kind of somersault in the air.

Altogether the day at the fair was splendid. In the evening George fixed supper for Dee. Then he went off to dinner with his cowboy friends. They got together at the big hotel in town and were about to sit down at a table when the proprietor spoke to George.

"You'll have to eat in the kitchen," he said.

Antine Meloche was there. Without a word, he got up from the table. The other men—George, too—followed him into the kitchen. A dozen cowboys all squeezed around a table near the stove, and the cook was frightened.

"We're eating here," Antine announced. "The boss in there told this friend of ours he couldn't sit in the dining room. We all eat together. Ain't that right?" Antine looked at the cowboys.

"That's right."

Very soon the proprietor changed his mind, and George, with his friends, ate in the dining room—at a table in the center.

CHAPTER 19

Last Days

George's story about the Bone Pit had fallen on interested ears when he told it to Carl Schwachheim in the blacksmith shop in Raton. But the blacksmith didn't find a way to get a ride to the Crowfoot Ranch forty miles away.

A few years later George talked to another man, Fred Howarth, who worked at the bank in Raton. Howarth, too, was a collector, and he was interested. He had once found the bones of a mammoth, a huge extinct elephant, and a friend had helped him preserve the tusk. Howarth said he'd like to look at the Bone Pit. But just as with Schwachheim, several years passed before he took a trip in that direction.

Meantime, George sold many of his cattle and began at last to build a house in Folsom. He felt that he was part of the town. There he acted as a kind of bridge between the Mexicans and the Anglos. His house even looked part Mexican and part Anglo. It had a strong stone foundation and Mexican-looking

George McJunkin as an old man.

walls, adobe-colored. But instead of building a flat Mexican roof, George had the house finished with an Anglo-style roof that sloped down four ways. "A roof like this sheds rain and snow," he explained to the men, both Mexican and Anglo, who worked for him.

To help pay for the house, George rented it and kept on living and working at the Crowfoot. The ranch demanded more of his time than ever because

Bill Jack had died and George was taking care of everything until Mrs. Jack could find someone to buy the place.

George himself might have been the buyer. He could have started payments by selling his house in Folsom. If he had bought the Crowfoot, he would have been his own boss for the first time in his life. But the chance came too late. He was an old man. His legs were giving him trouble. So he had to be satisfied with the freedom he had already achieved.

The buyer Mrs. Jack did find was Lud Shoemaker, father of Dee. Now once again George taught a young white boy all the skills of roping cattle and riding broncs. Once again he prepared a young man to deserve a set of silver spurs.

For a while he and Dee went to the Stuyvesant Springs Ranch near Capulin Mountain, where Crowfoot cattle were grazing. George, whose hair was white now, watched over Dee as Dee watched over the cattle.

There was a log cabin at Stuyvesant Springs, so George brought along many of his belongings—his fiddle and guitar and his books and his telescope. He planned to get his rock collection, the Indian skull, and the mysterious big bones sometime later. Just when, he couldn't be sure. Something was really wrong in George's body. He had to lean on a cane as he walked, and it was painful for him to ride.

Dee kept urging him to see Doc Steele. George promised he would the first time he could ride into Folsom. He knew the doctor, for he had often brought him loads of hay from the Crowfoot.

Before he got around to making a trip to town, a storm came up. This one was not nearly as bad as the cloudburst that brought the big flood to Folsom. But it broke George's heart. A bolt of lightning struck the roof of the log cabin and started a fire. George was inside at the time, but he escaped. He had always made a joke about lightning. "It never strikes a black man," he used to say.

George hobbled painfully from the cabin to the spring, then back, trying to put the fire out with buckets of water. It was no use. Before he could rescue his belongings, they were all burned.

Soon George was too ill to think of building a new cabin at Stuyvesant Springs. He couldn't even take care of himself in his own house in Folsom. He sold it to Mrs. Jack and went to live at the hotel.

There he lay in bed in a little back room and thought of many things. He thought of the slave world he had left and of the Promised Land he had found. In this beautiful valley were many bits and pieces of the freedom for which he had always hungered, but some elements of independence had always been beyond his reach. For one thing, he had never managed to be his own boss. Of course, most white cowboys, too, lived out their lives working for others, and those who did become ranchers sometimes got their start with stolen cattle. But although George had been a better cowboy than any of them, he had never reached his goal. He had always had to work for somebody who was born white and who somehow got money enough for a ranch.

Doc Steele visited George often as he lay in the little room. Friends dropped in to talk. After they left, he went back to his unfinished thoughts. Once more he wondered, as he often had in the past, about those puzzling bones he had found deep in Wild Horse Arroyo. But he never heard the answer to his questions. The great excitement about the bones came too late for him to enjoy. One night, before the importance of his discovery became known, George fell into a sleep from which he never awoke.

The next day, January 22, 1922, cowboys used their lariats to lower his coffin and buried George McJunkin in the Folsom cemetery. Some of those present at the funeral say that Mrs. White, who helped her husband run the drugstore, spoke a moving tribute to the great cowboy at his grave. No one recalls exactly the words she used, but she would have spoken the truth if she had said:

"George always thought of this valley as a place for freedom. He found much more of it here than he had known where he was born, although even here it was not complete. Nevertheless, the valley of the Dry Cimarron was the Promised Land to him. He always wished that other black people would join him, but they never did. And that probably is our fault. We didn't make them feel welcome.

"George loved people of every kind, children most of all, but he had no children of his own. Instead, he acted as a kind of father to all of us who grew up here.

"And George McJunkin himself kept growing as long as he lived. We are all more alive because of him."

CHAPTER 20

The Bone Pit Again

At exactly ten o'clock on the morning of July 1, 1922, Carl Schwachheim took off his leather apron and left the repair shop where he worked for the Santa Fe Railway in Raton, New Mexico. The hour had come when his union was going out on strike, and it looked as if the strike would be a long one. If it was, Carl now had time for something he had been dreaming of—a visit to George McJunkin's Bone Pit on the Crowfoot Ranch.

Carl still had no car, but Fred Howarth did. So the two of them planned a trip together.

Another man in Raton, James Campbell, a taxidermist, was deeply interested in natural science. The expedition to the Bone Pit had to include him.

Then there was their friend, Charles Bonahoom, a bricklayer from the far-off country of Lebanon. He asked to come along, and so did Father Roger Aull, the Roman Catholic priest in Raton.

By the time the expedition got organized, George

something like this. It
takes about 40 days for it to
come out of the ball.
Aug 13 Grama grass is in bloom
and is thick every where.
The Mesa picnic is today
Aug 18. Ants on a sunflower getting
honey from an insect
shaped something like this
only [drawing] about ¼
of an inch in length
The ants rub them & they
exude a small drop of honey
which the ant eats. There
were 3 different kinds of
ants after them. One so
small you can hardly see
them. It rains every day now
Aug 29 Scorpion with young on her
back they are very young yet.
There are 8 young. She helps
them on her back with her
arms & pincers. Caterpillars
on the skunkberry bush went
through a molt since last
night & came out with red-
heads this morning but are
black this evening. They are
eating all the leaves off of
the bush as they go. I found

an arrow point this morn-
ing it is of a clearcolored
agate or jasper. It is not
exposed the full length
but it is hollow on the
sides & looks some thing
like this [drawing] The point was
near a rib in the
matrix [drawing] One barb is
broken off. Since noon
Mr Blair found
another not in place
but in the loose dirt & is
much the same shape 1
inch [drawing] wide at break &
¾ [drawing] at base. Shaped
like this but more of
it Made of a dark red flint
These are not of the notched
points but are the link
between the spear or lance
& the notched points of a
later day. Sent a letter to
the boss today.
Aug 30 Small worms on the vines
with the berries growing
the porch they are about
an inch long with [...] 2
blue bands on each end Will
try to see what they make later

Part of the unpublished diary of Carl Schwachheim,
August 29, 1927. The drawings are probably the first
representations of Folsom Point.

McJunkin had been dead for several months. He would not have the satisfaction of seeing that people were at last paying attention to his discovery. However, although he was not there to guide the Raton party, the directions he had given were good. The men found the Bone Pit just where George had said it would be. They dug into the steep wall of the arroyo and took out a gunnysack full of specimens.

Back in Raton, James Campbell laid out some of their trophies on the kitchen table, and all evening he and Carl sat studying books, trying to find out what kind of animal the bones had come from. Was it a giant elk or a giant bison? Discussion went back and forth. They could settle the argument by consulting an expert at a museum, but there was no museum nearby. Unidentified, the bones remained in Raton for almost four years.

At last, in January, 1926, Fred Howarth had to deliver some cattle that his bank owned to the stockyards in Denver. He got Carl a job looking after the cattle during the train trip. Then they packed up some of their specimens, and on January 25, when the job with the cattle was over, they visited the Colorado Museum of Natural History.

The head of the museum, J. D. Figgins, knew a good deal about prehistoric animals. One look at the specimens told him that McJunkin's Bone Pit might be an important find.

Early in March, Figgins and another scientist traveled with Carl to the Crowfoot Ranch. What they saw in the Bone Pit was even more exciting than

Figgins had expected. There seemed to be many skeletons there, all belonging to a type of buffalo or bison that was new to science. No living man had ever seen animals of this kind, because they were extinct.

After the bison died, mud and gravel had washed down onto the spot from the hillside above and covered the bones. The skeletons were buried so deep in the earth that no one had seen them until George McJunkin found them after the flood. Under the thick layer of soil they had remained undisturbed for many thousands of years.

Perhaps a complete skeleton of this new type of bison could be unearthed at the Bone Pit. That was reason enough for the museum to excavate it. But Figgins had another reason. He hoped to find among the animal bones some evidence of human beings, too. A stone tool or weapon might show that a hunter, pursuing the bison, had been at this spot before the animals became extinct, a very, very long time ago. Figgins was one of the few scientists who believed that man must have been in America in very ancient times. Most of them believed that the earliest date was about three thousand years ago.

And so, when Figgins put Carl to work excavating the Bone Pit, he urged him to look out for any signs of man.

Carl began to remove the soil that covered the bones. He dug through ten feet of hard earth, and then one day he spied a small stone object. It looked like an arrowhead or the tip of a spear, but it had an unfamiliar shape.

This piece of stone delighted Figgins. He was sure it meant that men and bison had lived at the same time many thousands of years ago. But he also knew that other scientists would doubt the evidence. The stone spearpoint did not prove anything because Carl had found it in loose soil. He could not be sure exactly where it had come from. Perhaps it had slid down among the bones from the surface of the earth where some quite recent Indian had lost it.

Carl had to go on digging a second summer. Then, on August 2, 1927, came the discovery that he and Figgins had been hoping for. That morning Carl found a spearpoint that was tightly held in the earth. Most exciting of all, it was stuck between two bison ribs. The point and the ribs had lain together in that same spot ever since the bison died.

Carl immediately wrote a letter to J. D. Figgins reporting the great discovery. Then he drove a wagon in great haste to Folsom to put the letter on the evening train.

Experts came great distances to see the spearpoint still lying in the earth where Carl had found it. The evidence convinced them. Men had indeed been in America for many thousands of years—at least ten thousand.

Scientists renamed the Bone Pit the Folsom Site, after the nearby town. As more spearpoints appeared among the bones at the site, some of the experts began to wonder about the history of the place itself. They discovered that a black man had found it. Ultimately, it was he who had made possible a great advance in knowledge about the human past. Curious about his story, researchers then sought more details about the black cowboy who had had such a happy zest for living and for learning. They discovered George McJunkin—a most uncommon common man.

EPILOGUE

The Story of This Story

My search for information about George McJunkin began with some tape recordings that Dr. George A. Agogino of Eastern New Mexico University made when he interviewed two people who had known McJunkin. One of them was a cowboy named Upton Wilson. The other, Mrs. John J. Doherty at Hereford Park, was the granddaughter of Dr. Thomas Owen. Later Mrs. Doherty told me stories, showed me documents, lent me photographs, and sent written answers to many questions. Her husband had also known George McJunkin, and he told me very briefly how George had learned to ride.

Mrs. Doherty not only shared what she remembered, she also took my wife and me to the Crowfoot Ranch, which adjoins Hereford Park. There she showed us the site of the house where George lived and the workshop, still standing, in which he operated a forge, just as his father had done many years before. She led us to the graves of the Mingus

148

babies, where the rose George planted still bloomed, and she stood with us at the spot from which he first saw the big bison bones in Wild Horse Arroyo.

An article by Mrs. Doherty's uncle, Thomas E. Owen, published in the *Raton Daily Range* (June 28, 1951) led me to the back files of that paper. And in the town of Raton, I also found Tillie Schwachheim Burch.

Did Mrs. Burch remember how her brother Carl Schwachheim came to know about the bison bones? Indeed she did. She told the story of George's visit to the blacksmith shop where he noticed Carl's elk horns, and her son Thomas Burch arranged for me to have a copy of the photograph of Carl standing beside the horns. I am indebted to Tom and his mother for many other photographs, as well, and for the right to study and use Carl Schwachheim's unpublished diary.

Who else knew how word about the bison bones reached Raton? Mrs. Burch assured me that I could get help from Pearl C. Harnish, whose brother, James Campbell, had been in the party that followed up the report of McJunkin's Bone Pit. Mrs. Harnish not only remembered McJunkin's role, she also had a letter from Father Roger Aull confirming it.

Time after time, people referred me to Ivan Shoemaker, son of the rancher who bought the Crowfoot when George was an old man. Ivan, also known as Dee, was the last of a long series of white boys to whom George taught the arts of roping and peeling broncs. With zest he told me many a good story, and many of the details in them were confirmed by accounts in old newspapers and in public records. I hope my memory is as good as his when I reach his age.

Dee was generous in his admiration of McJunkin, and I have made generous use of the information he gave me. He also supplied information used by Jaxon Hewett, who wrote "The Bookish Black at Wild Horse Arroyo," which appeared in *New Mexico Magazine* (January-February, 1971). Anyone who reads that article will see that my researches led me to a rather different George McJunkin from the one Mr. Hewett found. Perhaps Mary Edmonston of Vista, California, is finding still another McJunkin. She, too, was stimulated by Dr. Agogino to study the black cowboy.

Several informants had varying ideas about where George was born. According to one account, he came from Missouri with Dr. Owen after the Civil War. The Missouri Historical Society could dig up nothing to support this story. They did find that Dr. Owen had been a Confederate officer, but there was no record that he had ever owned slaves.

Another account of George's origin had it that he came from Texas, where he worked first for one, then for another brother in a McJunkin family. One of these McJunkin men was known as Jack, and he ranched near Midland. However, Mary Edmonston disposed of Midland. That town, she discovered, had not been in existence at the time George would have worked there.

Still other clues pointed to Texas, and I decided to

follow them. Since black Americans often have surnames that came from the whites who owned their ancestors, I thought I might find out something about black George from surviving white McJunkins. One after another I wrote to people named McJunkin whose addresses I found in Texas telephone directories. And when I reached H. H. McJunkin, Sr., of Dallas, I hit pay dirt. This Mr. McJunkin was descended from a John Sanders McJunkin, and many a man named John has been called Jack. He and his brothers, I found later, lived not far from a Texas town called Mid*way.* According to family tradition, John Sanders McJunkin had a number of blacks on his ranch, where he raised horses and mules.

In an abandoned cemetery near Normangee, Texas, I found the grave of John Morrow McJunkin, a son of John Sanders McJunkin. Normangee, near the site of a town once called Rogers Prairie, is also in the vicinity of Midway and is on the border between Madison and Leon counties. The story, which came from Ivan Shoemaker, that George got his surname from a Jack McJunkin at Mid*land,* Texas, seems to be only a little bit askew.

Someday, I suspect, researchers in the records of Madison and Leon counties will find material that will throw additional light on the childhood of a remarkable black man who started life there at a difficult time. Researchers can start with a statement signed by George McJunkin that he was born in Texas in 1851. That statement appeared on papers he made out when he obtained a homestead, which is now incorporated in the Crowfoot Ranch. The papers came to me from the Bureau of Land Management files in Washington, D.C., through the courtesy of M. J. Romero in the Bureau's office in Santa Fe. I was led to look for them by Candido Archuletta, II, of Des Moines, New Mexico, who first told me of George's homestead and who later made a special trip to Santa Fe to get data I needed.

(Future researchers will also have to deal with the fact that after George's death the widow of Dr. Owen, who employed George, wrote on a card that George died January 21, 1922, at the age of 66 years, 12 days. This would have made his birthday January 9, 1856. For two reasons I used the 1851 date for George's birth rather than 1856: the 1851 date appears over George's own signature on a government record, and it was given at least twenty-one years before Mrs. Owen made her record, which was of necessity secondhand information.)

One more account will be enough to show how this book grew. In his story about George, which appeared in the *Raton Daily Range,* Thomas E. Owen said that George worked for Gid Roberds southeast of Trinidad, Colorado, before he worked for Dr. Owen. The name Roberds also turned up in an unpublished story about George in the Works Progress Administration Federal Writers Project archives in Santa Fe, which was sent to me by Dr. Myra Jenkins, New Mexico State Historian. But who was Roberds?

Ivan Shoemaker associated the name Roberds with

a special strain of quarter horse, the Peter McHugh. At this point my secretary, Judy Warren, who is interested in horses, suggested that a search through back files of the *Western Horseman* might reveal the whereabouts of a Roberds who raised Peter McHugh quarter horses. And Judy was right. She found that a Coke Roberds had indeed raised them in the 1940's near Hayden, Colorado.

Hayden is about as far from Trinidad as you can get and still be in Colorado, but I began the search for Coke Roberds. Telephone directories gave no help, so I wrote to the Mayor of Hayden. The letter was answered by Ruth W. Hofstetter, who gave me several leads to information about the late Coke Roberds. One of these took me ultimately to Lollie Milne in Tucson, Arizona. She was a granddaughter of Gideon Roberds and most lucid in her memories of the Roberds ranch and of family tradition.

At the same time Adrienne Anderson, who was doing archaeological work in the Folsom area, was becoming familiar with many local families and their history. She heard of a grandson of Gideon, Carl Roberds by name, who lived in Kimball, Nebraska. I wrote to Carl Roberds and got much colorful information about Gideon's journey to Colorado and the life of George McJunkin on the Roberds ranch.

Both Carl Roberds and Mrs. Milne agreed that Gideon Roberds had come originally from Georgia, and that he had reached Colorado by way of Texas. But where in Texas? Carl Roberds thought it was Comanche. Mrs. Milne thought it was Stephenville. Both towns lay on a route Roberds might well have taken from Waco on the Brazos, where Mrs. Milne said he lived for a while. Comanche, I learned, attained considerable notoriety for its maltreatment of blacks. In fact, there were no blacks living there several years ago, and perhaps not even today.

No blacks live in the vicinity of Folsom, New Mexico, either, and I could find none in all of northeastern New Mexico who had been there when George was alive and hence could have known him. My search had to be in the Anglo and Chicano communities.

From Mrs. Doherty came introductions to old-timers in both communities who had known George. Some of them, former residents in the Folsom area, had moved. Claude Goodson, once a sheriff in the town, now lived in Santa Fe. He had vivid recollections, and he sent me on to several people who gladly gave information and who sent me to still others. One was Mrs. Carl Hennegan, daughter of Dr. Steele, who took care of George in the last days of his life. Mrs. Hennegan had a pair of spurs that were a gift from George. So did Ivan Shoemaker and a number of others for whom George felt special affection.

If those who knew him do not always remember specific events in the same way, there is one thing on which almost all who have been interested in McJunkin agree: he was the kind of person who could set people to sharing. Most of us who have been studying him have shared with one another what we have found out. Some of us even met together in Folsom, New Mexico, on July 14, 1971, for a day's exchange of information.

Those who attended the meeting were Dr. Agogino and his wife, Dr. Mercedes Agogino; Dr. Morris F. Taylor, authority on local history, from Trinidad Junior College; Willard Louden of Bronson, Colorado, also a student of local history; Mary Germond, who is writing a book for adults based on the life of George McJunkin, and her husband, Dr. H. H. Germond; my wife, Mary Elting Folsom, who has shared in the research for this book; and finally Adrienne Anderson, a doctoral candidate in archaeology at the University of Colorado, who was making a minute study of the Folsom Site and who acted as our host. Mary Edmonston and her husband missed the meeting, but only because their car broke down.

Each of us at that gathering related our journeys, our interviews, our searches in libraries and public records, and we all went to Wild Horse Arroyo. There Adrienne Anderson showed us exactly where George McJunkin discovered the bison bones that changed the course of American archaeology.

The account of my own researches must include help I received in person from Emma Adams of the Folsom Museum; Dr. Alfred M. Bailey, Director, Denver Museum of Natural History; Margaret C. Blaker, National Anthropological Archives, Smithsonian Institution; Mrs. Murphy Bonahoom, Raton, New Mexico; the Reverend Ike Dodson, Normangee, Texas; Eula Edwards, San Jon, New Mexico; Will

Emory, Clayton, New Mexico; Homer Farr, Capulin, New Mexico; Felix Floyd, Springer, New Mexico; Thelma D. Fuller, Arthur Johnson Memorial Library, Raton; Greta Gallagher, Raton; Mrs. Tim Gillespie, Albuquerque, New Mexico; Pearl C. Harnish, Raton; Susie Henderson, Historical Society of New Mexico; Mr. and Mrs. Fred Honey, Folsom; Dorothy Jennings, New Mexico State Library, Santa Fe; Mrs. D. A. Johnson, Raton; Mary M. Johnson, National Archives; Kitty Lance, Osborn Library, American Museum of Natural History; Dr. E. B. Renaud, Denver; Dr. Joe Ben Wheat, University of Colorado.

My account also includes acknowledgment of help I received in the course of correspondence with the following: Dr. Herbert Aptheker, Director, Black Studies, Bryn Mawr College; Ben Beckner, County Clerk, Union County, New Mexico; Walter Briggs, Editor, *New Mexico;* Mrs. Kirk Bryan, Santa Fe; Dr. Kirk Bryan, Jr., Princeton, New Jersey; A. P. Burks, Burks Museum, Comanche, Texas; Dorothy J. Caldwell, Associate Editor, *Missouri Historical Review;* Harry E. Chrisman, Denver; Bruce T. Ellis, Museum of New Mexico; W. Peyton Fawcett, Librarian, Field Museum of Natural History; Naomi Harker, Reference Service, the Genealogical Society of the Church of Latter-Day Saints; Mrs. A. V. Kidder, Cambridge, Massachusetts; A. D. Mastrogiuseppe, Jr., Western Historical Collection, University of Colorado; C. Boone McClure, Director, The Panhandle Plains Historical Society, Canyon, Texas; Arthur Mitchell, Pioneer Museum, Trinidad; D. D. Monroe, Clayton,

New Mexico; W. L. More, Vice President, Personnel, The Atchison, Topeka and Santa Fe Railway; James Morrow, Raton; Dorothy Nordyke, *Amarillo Daily News;* Dr. Phil C. Orr, Santa Barbara, California; Dorothy B. Porter, Librarian, Negro Collection, Howard University Library; Evelyn P. Semoton, Steamboat Springs, Colorado; Mrs. J. K. Shiskin, History Library, Museum of New Mexico; Clyde Sowers, Publisher, *Union County Leader,* Clayton; Virginia Lee Starkey, Reference Librarian, Historical Society of Colorado; Janet A. Stoker, New Mexico State Records Center and Archives; Paul Ton, Denver; Ted L. Whitener, Ordinary, Gilmer County, Georgia; Dr. Edwin N. Wilmsen, University of Michigan; Dr. H. M. Wormington, Denver.

In gathering information I also made use of publications, including the following: Richard Bardolph, *The Negro Vanguard,* Rinehart, 1959; Harry E. Chrisman, *Lost Trails of the Cimarron,* Sage Books, 1961; *Trinidad* [Colorado] *Chronicle-News,* February 9, 1930; Mrs. N. H. Click, *Us Nesters in the Land of Enchantment,* Des Moines, N. M.; Philip Durham and Everett Jones, *The Negro Cowboy,* Dodd Mead, 1963; James E. Haley, *Charles Goodnight, Cowman and Plainsman,* University of Oklahoma Press, 1949; Clara T. Harvey, *Not So Wild the Old West,* Clayton, N.M.; W. L. Katz, *Eyewitness: The Negro in American History,* Pitman, New York, 1967; *New Mexico Brand Book, 1915,* Cattle Sanitary Board, Santa Fe; C. W. Ramsdell, *Reconstruction in Texas,* University of Texas Press, 1970; *Raton Daily Range,* various issues; Sister Blandina Segal, *At the End of the Santa Fe Trail,* Bruce Publishing Co., Milwaukee; F. Stanley, *The Folsom* [New Mexico] *Story* and *The Johnson Mesa Story,* Pep, Texas; Morris F. Taylor, *Trinidad, Colorado Territory,* Trinidad State Junior College; Mrs. Harry Thompson, *History of Clayton and Union County, N.M.,* Monitor Publishing Co., Denver, 1962; Albert W. Thompson, *They Were Open Range Days,* World Press, Denver, 1946.

For help in preparing the list of books for further reading about black pioneers in the West and about discoveries of early man, I am indebted to Betty Bacon, Supervisor of Children's Services, Vallejo Public Library, Vallejo, California.

To all who helped in the search I am very grateful.

For reading my manuscript and advising me about it I am very grateful to Mrs. Ethel Richard, Middle School Librarian, Mahwah, New Jersey, and Selector, Bro-Dart Elementary School Library Collection; and to Mrs. Mildred Walter, author of *Lillie of Watts* and *Lillie of Watts Takes a Giant Step.*

For any errors of fact or interpretation none of those who have helped me can be held responsible.

Bibliography

Some Books About Black Pioneers on the Frontier

Durham, Philip, and Everett L. Jones. *Adventures of the Negro Cowboys.* New York, Dodd, Mead, 1966.

Felton, Harold W. *Edward Rose: Negro Trail Blazer.* New York, Dodd, Mead, 1967.

_____*Jim Beckwourth, Negro Mountain Man.* New York, Dodd, Mead, 1966.

_____*Nat Love, Negro Cowboy.* New York, Dodd, Mead, 1969.

Heard, Joseph Norman. *The Black Frontiersmen: Adventures of Negroes Among American Indians, 1528-1918.* New York, John Day, 1969.

Place, Marian T. *Rifles and War Bonnets.* New York, Ives Washburn, 1968.

Wormser, Richard. *The Black Mustanger.* New York, William Morrow, 1971. (Fiction).

Some Books About the Discovery of Early Man in America

Kirk, Ruth. *The Oldest Man in America: An Adventure in Archeology.* New York, Harcourt Brace Jovanovich, 1970.

Lauber, Patricia. *Who Discovered America? Settlers and Explorers of the New World Before the Time of Columbus.* New York, Random House, 1970.

Marriott, Alice. *The First Comers: Indians in America's Dawn.* New York, Longmans, Green, 1960.

Scheele, William E. *The Earliest Americans.* New York, World Publishing Company, 1963.

Suggs, Robert C. *Modern Discoveries in Archeology.* New York, Thomas Y. Crowell, 1962.

Vlahos, Olivia. *New World Beginnings: Indian Cultures in the Americas.* New York, Viking Press, 1970.

Index